Experiencing Jesus through the Eyes of the Samaritan Woman

What This Story Can Teach Us
About Missional Living

John 4:1–42

Patrick Sawyer

ISBN 979-8-88943-983-7 (hardcover)
ISBN 979-8-88943-984-4 (digital)

Copyright © 2024 by Patrick Sawyer

All rights reserved. No part of this publication may be reproduced, distributed, or transmitted in any form or by any means, including photocopying, recording, or other electronic or mechanical methods without the prior written permission of the publisher. For permission requests, solicit the publisher via the address below.

Christian Faith Publishing
832 Park Avenue
Meadville, PA 16335
www.christianfaithpublishing.com

Printed in the United States of America

Contents

Introduction v
Chapter 1: Who Was the Samaritan Woman? 1
Chapter 2: Jesus Was Intentional 5
Chapter 3: Jesus Listened 34
Chapter 4: Jesus Showed Love and Compassion 42
Chapter 5: Jesus Fellowshipped 53
Chapter 6: Jesus Was truthful 79
Chapter 7: Jesus Changed Her Life 106
Chapter 8: Jesus Shared His Time 118
Chapter 9: Conclusion 127
Bibliography 135

Introduction

I attended a conference on how to become a sending church hosted by Hope Church in Las Vegas, Nevada, which was then pastored by Vance Pittman. During one session, Pittman shared how, when he and his team set foot on the ground in Las Vegas to plant a church, one of the first important things they did was to decide to study the life of Jesus through the gospels. Pittman stated that this was one of the best things they did, and he encouraged us to one day go through the gospels and just study all that Jesus did: how Jesus engaged with the disciples, how he engaged with the religious leaders, and also, how he engaged with everyday people. As I thought about this challenge, it got me thinking, how did Jesus engage in evangelism?

As Christians, we are called to the Great Commission. Matthew 28:18–20 states,

> And Jesus came and said to them, "All authority in heaven and on earth has been given to me. Go therefore and make disciples of all nations, baptizing them in the name of the Father and of the Son and of the Holy Spirit, teaching them to observe all that I have commanded you. And behold, I am with you always, to the end of the age." (ESV)

As you study the Great Commission, the verb is make. We are to make disciples of all nations, and a part of making disciples is sharing the good news of the gospel. As I thought about what Vance

Pittman said, again, I thought if we look at the life and ministry of Jesus, how did he share the truth of the gospel with others?

One of my favorite stories in the Bible is the story of Jesus and the woman at the well in John 4:1–42. As I have studied this story more and more and taught on it many times, I personally believe it is one of the best examples of how to properly engage with people with the intent of building relationships that lead to gospel conversations. Why do I think this story is a good model for us? Because in this story, Jesus does not heal anyone or exorcise a demon out of anyone. All Jesus did was what you and I can do every day, and that is to intentionally build relationships with people that prayerfully lead to gospel conversations.

In the book *The Gospel Conversation*, Steve Gaines stated, "People are talking. Conversations are taking place everywhere, all the time. People communicate one-on-one and also in groups. While the content of many conversations is shallow, conversations nevertheless are continuous."[1] He goes on to say, "The most important conversations are those that focus on the gospel of Jesus Christ. Gospel conversations are the vehicles God uses to communicate His saving truths of: God's love for man, man's need for God, man's sinful state, Jesus sacrificial atonement, repentance and faith, and the need to receive Christ by calling on His name in prayer."[2]

As Christians, we are called to the Great Commission, which means we are all called to engage in gospel conversations. In Mark 1:17, Jesus called Simon and Andrew to follow Him, and He would make them fishers of men. This was not an option. To follow Jesus is to be a fishers of men. Harvey Turner stated, "It's pretty simple: fishermen fish. Disciples of Jesus evangelize. Disciples make disciples. So whatever your vision of the Christian life is, it must include evangelism as its mission."[3] Jerram Barrs, in the book *Learning Evangelism From Jesus*, reminds us that Jesus desires for His people to be like

---

[1] Sam Greer, *The Gospel Conversation: Engaging the Lost in Everyday Life* (Replicate, 2017), vii.
[2] Ibid.
[3] Harvey Turner, *Friends of Sinners: An Approach to Evangelism* (Houston, TX: Lucid Books, 2016), 12.

EXPERIENCING JESUS THROUGH THE EYES OF THE SAMARITAN WOMAN

Him and to engage the nonbelieving world and develop intimate relationships with them for the sake of the gospel of Jesus.[4] If we, as Christians, want to truly learn how to engage the world with gospel conversations, then we must, like Pittman said, study how the Master did it. Jesus is truly the model evangelist, and I believe we can learn a lot from Him by studying this story and how Jesus engaged this woman with a gospel conversation. Barrs stated, "It is my deep conviction that our evangelism, both in theory and practice, must be shaped not only by the general teaching of Scripture but also, indeed most of all, by imitating the pattern of Christ."[5]

The purpose of this book is twofold. First is to look deeply into this story from the perspective of the Samaritan woman to see how Jesus engaged her with the intent of sharing the truth of the gospel with her. This book will reveal how Jesus approached her, how He started a general conversation with her, and how He intentionally led her from a general conversation to a spiritual conversation. This book will reveal how this woman's life was radically changed through her experience with Jesus as He engaged her through intentionality, through love and compassion, through fellowship, and finally, through truth. Most books on evangelism focus on the disciples of Jesus as they engage the world with the gospel, but where this book is different is that is focuses on evangelism from the perspective of the person being engaged, such as the Samaritan woman in this story. I believe this story from her eyes will give us more confidence as we, as Christians, go out, live on a mission, and engage the world with the gospel of Jesus.

When Jesus finished this conversation, there was no doubt in the woman's mind who Jesus was and that He was the promised Messiah that God promised to Adam and Eve back in the garden when they ate the forbidden fruit and brought sin into the world (Genesis 3). Genesis 3:15 states, "I will put enmity between you and the woman, and between your offspring and her offspring; he shall bruise your

---

[4] Jerram Barrs, *Learning Evangelism From Jesus* (Wheaton, IL: Crossway, 2009), 14.
[5] Jerram Barrs, *Learning Evangelism From Jesus* (Wheaton, IL: Crossway, 2009), 15.

head, and you shall bruise his heel." After this, God, in His love and grace, promised Adam and Eve that He would one day send a Redeemer; Savior, who would come and make right what sin had made wrong and who would come and redeem God's people back to Himself. This promised Messiah is Jesus Christ, and the woman at the well left her encounter with Jesus with no doubt that this man who had approached her about water is the promised Redeemer who was to come. We see this in John 4:25–26: "The woman said to him, 'I know that Messiah is coming (he who is called Christ). When he comes, he will tell us all things.' Jesus said to her, 'I who speak to you am he.'" Verses 28–29 says, "So the woman left her water jar and went away into town and said to the people, 'Come, see a man who told me all that I ever did. Can this be the Christ?'" John MacArthur stated,

> So profound was Jesus impact on her that she did not hesitate to share the news about Him—even those familiar with her sordid reputation. Jesus had read her heart and forced her to face who she really was. She had already recognized her need (v15), her sin (v19), her true condition (v26) and that He was the source of her eternal life. Now she eagerly desired to communicate her discovery to others. Her zeal and enthusiasm provides the clinching piece of evidence that her conversion was genuine.[6]

The story goes on to say how many people believed because of her testimony, and they asked Jesus to stay with them and, after spending time with Jesus, they knew He was the Messiah who was to come. This woman knew the promised Messiah would know all things and when Jesus shared with her all about her, I believe she knew He was the promised Messiah. As Christians, as we go out and

---

[6] John MacArthur, *The MacArthur New Testament Commentary: John 1–11* (Chicago, IL: Moody Publishers, 2006), 156.

EXPERIENCING JESUS THROUGH THE EYES
OF THE SAMARITAN WOMAN

engage the world and share the truth of the gospel, my prayer is that we leave people with no doubt who Jesus is and that He is the only one who can truly save us, satisfy us, reconcile us back to God and give us life, now and for eternity.

Second, this book will reveal how Jesus is our model evangelist and if we, as His disciples, would follow His example of how He engaged this woman with the gospel, this beautiful story is a perfect example of how Christians can engage the world with the good news of the gospel through intentional relationships that lead to gospel conversations following the model that Jesus has provided His people through His Word. Each chapter will focus on a different way Jesus engaged this woman, through the eyes of this woman, and will then provide practical ways Christians can model Jesus' example in order to build intentional relationships that lead to gospel conversations. My prayer for this book is that Christians may read this book, study this story, watch how Jesus engaged this woman from her perspective, and put this book down walking away with a more confident example and plan for future gospel conversations.

Matthew 24:14 states, "And this gospel of the kingdom will be proclaimed throughout the whole world as a testimony to all nations, and then the end will come." If God's plan, which we know it is, is to spread His kingdom through the proclamation of His people then His people must be obedient to His command (Matthew 28:18–20) and start going, proclaiming the gospel and making disciples and it starts with engaging the world with the purpose of building intentional relationships that lead to gospel conversations. There is no better way or better example, I believe, than Jesus and His encounter with the woman from Samaria.

Before we move forward, if by chance you have picked up this book and you may be exploring Christianity and are not a follower of Jesus, please do not put this book down. This book is for you as well. My prayer is that as you read this story, you will also experience Jesus just like this woman did. How she experienced Jesus' love and compassion when it seems like no one else cared for her. This woman was so joyful after her experience with Jesus that she ran into her village where the people wanted nothing to do with her and told them to go and meet this Jesus. Her actions revealed her experience with this Jesus who she believed was the promised Messiah that would come. I share her excitement and her belief in that Jesus is the Savior of the world.

I hope that through this story, you know the real Jesus who truly does love you and who loves you so much that He came and died for you on the cross and rose from the dead so that you can have true joy, satisfaction, and life now and for eternity. I hope you also understand how much Jesus loves you that He sends His people out into the world to share the truth about Him to you and the world. That is my prayer for you. My challenge is for you to continue reading and experience the real Jesus. The one who can truly give you the joy you are searching for, the peace that you are longing for, and the hope that you desire.

John 4:1–42

As we begin this journey, when I teach on missional living, one of the most exciting things I do is to have students or church members read the entire story and then take ten minutes and write down everything you see Jesus do as He engages this woman. I would encourage you at this time to do just this. Read the entire story and then take ten minutes and write down everything you see Jesus do as He engages this woman. I would also encourage you to think through and write down ways you can engage the world following Jesus' example. Do this before you proceed any further in this book.

Welcome back! I hope you have read the story, wrote down all you saw Jesus do, and then also wrote down ideas of how you can follow His example as you live on mission and engage the world. Now as we continue this book, let's start by reading this story together. Here is the story of Jesus and the Samaritan woman.

> Now when Jesus learned that the Pharisees had heard that Jesus was making and baptizing more disciples than John (although Jesus himself

EXPERIENCING JESUS THROUGH THE EYES OF THE SAMARITAN WOMAN

did not baptize, but only his disciples), he left Judea and departed again for Galilee. And he had to pass through Samaria. So he came to a town of Samaria called Sychar, near the field that Jacob had given to his son Joseph. Jacob's well was there; so Jesus, wearied as he was from his journey, was sitting beside the well. It was about the sixth hour. A woman from Samaria came to draw water. Jesus said to her, "Give me a drink." (For his disciples had gone away into the city to buy food.) The Samaritan woman said to him, "How is it that you, a Jew, ask for a drink from me, a woman of Samaria?" (For Jews have no dealings with Samaritans.)

Jesus answered her, "If you knew the gift of God, and who it is that is saying to you, 'Give me a drink,' you would have asked him, and he would have given you living water." The woman said to him, "Sir, you have nothing to draw water with, and the well is deep. Where do you get that living water? Are you greater than our father Jacob? He gave us the well and drank from it himself, as did his sons and his livestock."

Jesus said to her, "Everyone who drinks of this water will be thirsty again, but whoever drinks of the water that I will give him will never be thirsty again. The water that I will give him will become in him a spring of water welling up to eternal life." The woman said to him, "Sir, give me this water, so that I will not be thirsty or have to come here to draw water." Jesus said to her, "Go, call your husband, and come here." The woman answered him, "I have no husband." Jesus said to her, "You are right in saying, 'I have no husband'; for you have had five husbands, and the one you now have is not your husband. What you have said is true."

The woman said to him, "Sir, I perceive that you are a prophet. Our fathers worshiped on this mountain, but you say that in Jerusalem is the place where people ought to worship." Jesus said to her, "Woman, believe me, the hour is coming when neither on this mountain nor in Jerusalem will you worship the Father. You worship what you do not know; we worship what we know, for salvation is from the Jews. But the hour is coming, and is now here, when the true worshipers will worship the Father in spirit and truth, for the Father is seeking such people to worship him. God is spirit, and those who worship him must worship in spirit and truth."

The woman said to him, "I know that Messiah is coming (he who is called Christ). When he comes, he will tell us all things." Jesus said to her, "I who speak to you am he." Just then his disciples came back. They marveled that he was talking with a woman, but no one said, "What do you seek?" or, "Why are you talking with her?"

So the woman left her water jar and went away into town and said to the people, "Come, see a man who told me all that I ever did. Can this be the Christ?" They went out of the town and were coming to him. Meanwhile the disciples were urging him, saying, "Rabbi, eat." But he said to them, "I have food to eat that you do not know about." So the disciples said to one another, "Has anyone brought him something to eat?"

Jesus said to them, "My food is to do the will of him who sent me and to accomplish his work.

EXPERIENCING JESUS THROUGH THE EYES OF THE SAMARITAN WOMAN

Do you not say, 'There are yet four months, then comes the harvest'? Look, I tell you, lift up your eyes, and see that the fields are white for harvest. Already the one who reaps is receiving wages and gathering fruit for eternal life, so that sower and reaper may rejoice together. For here the saying holds true, 'One sows and another reaps.' I sent you to reap that for which you did not labor. Others have labored, and you have entered into their labor."

Many Samaritans from that town believed in him because of the woman's testimony, "He told me all that I ever did." So when the Samaritans came to him, they asked him to stay with them, and he stayed there two days. And many more believed because of his word. They said to the woman, "It is no longer because of what you said that we believe, for we have heard for ourselves, and we know that this is indeed the Savior of the world."

1

Who Was the Samaritan Woman?

We do not really know a lot about this woman because she is only mentioned in the Bible in this one story. Obviously, we know she was a Samaritan. Who were the Samaritans? When the northern ten tribes were carried into captivity to Assyria, the king sent people from Cutha, Ava, Hamath, and Sephravaim to inhabit Samaria, which was the capital city. These Gentiles would start to intermarry with the Jews, have offspring, and create the Samaritans.

We also know she seemed to have been isolated from the rest of her village.

> So he came to a town of Samaria called Sychar, near the field that Jacob had given to his son Joseph. Jacob's well was there; so Jesus, wearied as he was from his journey, was sitting beside the well. It was about the sixth hour. A woman from Samaria came to draw water. Jesus said to her, "give me a drink." (John 4:5–7)

The sixth hour would have been around noon and also would have been the hottest part of the day. Most women would have come to draw water early in the morning or later in the evening during the cooler parts of the day.[7] This would have been a very social time for the women so many of them would go together. DA Carson stated, "Women were more likely to come in groups to fetch water, and either earlier or later in the day when the heat of the sun was not so fierce."[8] This would be their Starbucks. But this woman would come during the hottest part of the day where she would be alone, and so it seemed that this woman was not accepted by her own people. John Macarthur reveals not only did this woman come during the hottest part of the day, but she also traveled a long distance to this specific well and passed over closer water sources.[9] He goes on to reveal that she would rather had walked a longer distance in the hotter part of the day than face the women she would encounter at a closer well in a cooler part of the day. Chris Anderson, in his book *The God Who Satisfies*, stated, "Solitude and sunburn were nothing compared to the whispers and dirty looks that must have come from at least five groups of mothers, sisters, and current wives. This woman was an outcast among outcasts."[10]

Even though we do not know a lot about her personally, I believe she represents many problems in our society today. Chris Anderson stated, "This story points to the answers for so many problems of our own day, such as racial prejudice, religious confusion, materialism, divorce and sensuality."[11] Her first problem was her race. We already stated this, but this woman was a Samaritan. The Jews hated the Samaritans. Barrs stated, "In Jesus' time the Jews hated the Samaritans even more than they despised 'pure' Gentiles, for they regarded them as polluting the blood of the patriarchs."[12] This is why

---

[7] Jerram Barrs, *Learning Evangelism From Jesus* (Wheaton, IL: Crossway, 2009), 40.
[8] DA Carson, *The Gospel According to John* (Grand Rapids, MI: Eerdmans Publishing, 1991), 217.
[9] John MacArthur, *The MacArthur New Testament Commentary: John 1–11* (Chicago, IL: Moody Publishers, 2006), 143.
[10] Chris Anderson, *The God Who Satisfies: How Jesus Seeks, Saves and Satisfies Samaritan Woman-Like Us* (Church Works, 2016), 12.
[11] Ibid.
[12] Jerram Barrs, *Learning Evangelism From Jesus* (Wheaton, IL: Crossway, 2009), 38.

in verse 9, the women was surprised that Jesus, who was a Jew, would have approached her, a Samaritan.

Her second problem was her religion. The religion of the Samaritans was a mixture between the true God of Israel and pagan idolatry practiced by the people from Babylon who had been sent there by the Assyrians.[13] Where Jerusalem worshiped in the temple at Jerusalem, the Samaritans worshiped in their temple built on Mt. Gerizim. Verses 19–20 state, "The women said to him, 'Sir, I perceive that you are a prophet. Our fathers worshiped on this mountain, but you say that in Jerusalem is the place where people ought to worship.'"

Her third problem was that she was divorced. Verses 16–18 state, "Jesus said to her, 'Go, call your husband, and come here.' The women answered him, 'I have no husband.' Jesus said to her, 'you are right you have no husband, for you have had five husbands, and the one you now have is not your husband. What you said is true.'" Because this women had been divorced this many times, she would have been excommunicated by everyone.

Her fourth problem was she was involved in sexual sin. Jesus knew she was now living with a man who was not her husband. According to Barrs, this woman would have been viewed by other women as a women who has been passed from man to man, and she would have been seen as a threat to their marriages.[14]

Her fifth problem was that she was engaged in materialism. Materialism is when we try to find something material to comfort us rather than spiritual values. Verse 13 says, "Jesus said to her, 'everyone who drinks of this water will be thirsty again.'" This women was finding her comfort in men and sex and Jesus was telling her that she can continue to seek and seek in material things, but these things will never satisfy us.

When it comes to the Samaritan woman, Anderson stated, "This unnamed lady is representative of everybody. We all experi-

---

[13] Ibid., 38.
[14] Jerram Barrs, *Learning Evangelism From Jesus* (Wheaton, IL: Crossway, 2009), 40.

ence painful solitude. We all have skeletons in our closets. We all have more questions than answers. And we all have a deep thirst for something more—even if we don't know what that something is."[15] What we learn from this woman is that no matter who you are—rich or poor, religious or secular, Republican or Democrat, no matter your ethnicity, we all need Jesus. Jesus is the only one who can truly bring us joy, satisfaction, salvation, peace, hope, and life. Jesus told this woman that she can continue to drink her water, and she will never be quenched, but the water that Jesus brings will fully quench our thirst.

As this woman represents everybody and the many problems we see in the world today, as Christians, as we go out into the world and encounter people and these problems in our society, such as racism, religious pluralism, sexual impurity, divorce, and materialism, we must understand they all need Jesus. Martin Luther stated, "A gospel that does not address the issues of the day is not the gospel at all."[16] The only true solution to these problems is the gospel of Jesus Christ. JC Ryle stated, "We must never despise of any soul after reading this passage. None can be worse than this woman. But Christ did not despise her. We must never despair of any soul after reading this passage. If this woman was converted, anyone may be converted."[17] So how do we engage people and these issues with the truth of the gospel? I am glad you asked. Jesus has given us the model, so how did Jesus do it? Continue reading to find out.

---

[15] Chris Anderson, *The God Who Satisfies: How Jesus Seeks, Saves and Satisfies Samaritan Woman-Like Us* (Church Works, 2016), 13.
[16] Larry Sharp, *Missions Disrupted* (Peabody, MA: Hendrickson Publishing, 2022), 17.
[17] JC Ryle, *Expository Thoughts On The Gospels*. Vol. 3 (Grand Rapids, MI: Baker Books, 2007), 227.

2

Jesus Was Intentional

> So he told them this parable: "What man of you, having a hundred sheep, if he has lost one of them, does not leave the ninety-nine in the open country, and go after the one that is lost, until he finds it? And when he has found it, he lays it on his shoulders, rejoicing. And when he comes home, he calls together his friends and his neighbors, saying to them, 'Rejoice with me, for I have found my sheep that was lost.' Just so, I tell you, there will be more joy in heaven over one sinner who repents than over ninety-nine righteous persons who need no repentance." (Luke 15:3–7)

I can remember like it was yesterday, I was sitting in my evangelism class in seminary, and one of the assignments we had to do was to have intentional gospel encounters every week throughout the semester. One of the most important truths I learned during this assignment was the importance of being intentional. I learned that in order for us to build relationships with the hopes of having gospel conversations, we must be very intentional. If we are not intentional with gospel engagements, they will never happen. I also learned that in order for us to be intentional with gospel engagements, we must always be open to the Spirit and where God is working and allow

Him to lead us and use us for His work. In the book *Recapturing Evangelism*, Matt Queen stated,

> Some believers assume they should wait for God to provide them evangelism opportunities. Advocates of this view determine they will wait expectantly for the Holy Spirit to generate the perfect circumstance or situation that will prompt them to evangelize. An example of such an opportunity entails believers waiting until unbelievers randomly at the Spirit's prompting, ask them about Christianity, the gospel, Jesus, or some other spiritual matter before they share the gospel with them.[18]

I agree with Queen in that we must be proactive when it comes to evangelism. I believe God can and will sometimes give us these "perfect" opportunities where someone may bring up a question or conversation about religion, Christianity or anything spiritual, but I would say this is not the norm. So if you are sitting around waiting on an unbeliever to knock on your door or approach you in public and ask you to share the gospel with them, you will probably be waiting your whole life. We must be proactive when it comes to evangelism. We must always be looking for opportunities to share the gospel.

I believe we see Jesus do this. In John 5:19, Jesus says these words: "So Jesus said to them, 'Truly, truly, I say to you, the Son can do nothing of his own accord, but only what he sees the Father doing. For whatever the Father does, that the Son does likewise.'" As Jesus was engaged in His ministry, He was led by the Spirit and the Father revealed to Him where He was working and the Spirit led Jesus to do what He saw the Father doing and was calling Jesus to do. Jesus saw where the Father was working, and He was obedient by joining His Father's work.

---

[18] Matt Queen, *Recapturing Evangelism* (Brentwood, TN: B&H Publishing, 2023), 14–15.

EXPERIENCING JESUS THROUGH THE EYES OF THE SAMARITAN WOMAN

At the same time that I was taking the evangelism class and trying to be intentional with engaging people with gospel conversations, I met a guy at my gym. As I met this guy and started to get to know him, I started to be more intentional with him. We started meeting at the same time at the gym and would work out together. One day, we met up for lunch and got to know each other better. We learned about each other's families and each other's jobs, among other things. I learned how he was in the car insurance business, and he learned I was working for Powerade at the time, but I was also highly involved in my church. At that lunch, I invited him to my church, but he never came.

One day, as I was wanting to be more intentional with him, I invited him to lunch again. I can remember like it was yesterday because I remember how nervous I was. I had told myself and my wife that I was going to share the gospel with him if I had the opportunity. All the way to the restaurant, I can just remember praying to God to give me an opportunity, to also give me confidence, and more importantly, to make it easy to share the gospel. As I got to the restaurant and we started eating and talking, the restaurant got really loud, so I started to get disappointed and began to pray that the Lord would give me courage and help me and again give me an easy opportunity.

About that time, the restaurant started to thin out, and it went from very loud to almost dead silent, and then I can remember thinking and praying, *Lord, please show me and give me a way to transition to the gospel.* I think it is funny that I am writing this book about this story with Jesus and the Samaritan woman because in this moment, I remember thinking of this story and how Jesus went from everyday plain water to the gospel. I also remember thinking, *Lord, give me my opportunity to go from a water conversation to a gospel conversation*, and then about that time, I heard these beautiful words from my friend when he said, "Tell me how things are going in your church." In volleyball terms, God gave me the perfect set for me to spike down. I remember thinking, *Boom! Lord, you made this too easy.* God gave me my water moment, and now it was my time to transition to a gospel conversation. It was at this time that I shared with him how much

God had done for me and my family and how good God was and then eventually led to me sharing the gospel with my friend. Now I will go on to tell you that even as I write this book, my friend has not accepted Jesus as his Lord and Savior. To this day, I continue to pray for him.

I share this story because the only reason I believe this happened was because I was very intentional. I was intentional when I invited him to lunch, and I was intentional in that I was prepared and planned to share the gospel with him if the Lord opened up the door. The truth is that if we want to engage people to build relationships that lead to gospel conversations, then we must be very intentional. I am not saying God cannot work in other ways and maybe sometimes He does, but I believe, for the most part, we must be intentional with people if we really want to build a relationship with them, and we must always be open, willing, and watching for God to open up the door to share the gospel; and then when He does open the door, we must be obedient. Matt Queen states again,

> Evangelism does not happen incidentally. It occurs intentionally. Intentionality in evangelism is not simply knowing you should evangelize, rather it is constructing a plan to evangelize consistently and executing it. To practice consistent evangelism, it must be planned—whether into daily, weekly, and/or monthly calendar events, or planned obedience in those moments of unscheduled prompting by the Holy Spirit.[19]

Queen goes on to say, "Evangelism will never occur by accident. It may take place during times and at places believers neither expect nor anticipate, but it will never occur until and unless they actually decide to evangelize."[20]

---

[19] Matt Queen, *Recapturing Evangelism* (Brentwood, TN: B&H Publishing, 2023), 17.
[20] Ibid.

EXPERIENCING JESUS THROUGH THE EYES OF THE SAMARITAN WOMAN

When it comes to being intentional, I believe we see Jesus be very intentional in this story. Why do I say Jesus was intentional?

> Now when Jesus learned that the Pharisees had heard that Jesus was making and baptizing more disciples than John (although Jesus himself did not baptize, but only his disciples), he left Judea and departed again for Galilee. And he had to pass through Samaria. So he came to a town of Samaria called Sychar, near the field that Jacob had given to his son Joseph. Jacob's well was there; so Jesus, wearied as he was from his journey, was sitting beside the well. It was about the sixth hour. (John 4:1–6)

This passage stated, "Jesus had to pass through Samaria." Did Jesus have to pass through Samaria? Remember, during this time, the Jews hated the Samaritans, so the Jews would have done anything possible to not pass through Samaria; if there were anyway for a Jew to go from Judea back to Galilee without going through Samaria, they would have for sure taken that route. According to Barrs, the only way a Jew would have went through Samaria were if they were in a hurry, but Jesus was not in a hurry because, not only did He go through Samaria, but He also stayed in Sychar for two extra days (verse 40).[21] The truth is that Jesus did not have to pass through Samaria. There were in fact three different routes Jesus could have taken. First, a Jew could have journeyed inland following the Jordan River. Second, a Jew could have gone by the coast road along the Mediterranean to the west. Third, a Jew could have taken the fastest route, which would have been through Samaria as Jesus did. Even though going through Samaria would have been the fastest route, a Jew would have not taken this route unless they absolutely had to. John MacArthur stated,

---

[21] Jerram Barrs, *Learning Evangelism From Jesus* (Wheaton, IL: Crossway, 2009), 36.

> The road through Samaria was shorter than the coastal road or the road on the east side of the Jordan, which is why many Jews traveled on it, especially at the time of the major religious festivals. But so great was their disdain for the Samaritans that the stricter Jews avoided traveling through Samaria altogether. They preferred instead to be defiled by a lesser evil, thus they would cross the Jordan and travel up its east banks through the largely Gentile regions of Perea. They would then cross back into Galilee north of Samaria. Jesus could have easily gone that way.[22]

If most Jews would not have come the way Jesus did and stayed the way Jesus did, why did Jesus? Because He had a divine appointment with a special someone.

I was talking to a church planter one time, and he told me how one of the ways he lives on mission and engages his community is that he goes to a coffee shop and just sits there until the Lord gives him the opportunity to strike up a conversation with someone with the intent of a gospel conversation. The planter told me that when he walks us to someone, he asks them if they are his appointment for the day. When they looked confused and told him he must be mistaken, he told them they are his divine appointment that God has orchestrated. I am not indicating that if you're reading this that you do this, but you have to admire his intentionality and strategy.

The reason Jesus had to pass through Samaria was because He was eager to meet this specific woman. Jesus was being obedient to the Father in that He was living on mission and taking the gospel from Jerusalem, Judea, Samaria, and to the ends of the world (Acts 1:8). Verses 31–38 reveal the disciples had left, and while Jesus was engaging this woman, they came back and asked Jesus if He had eaten. Look at

---

[22] John MacArthur, *The MacArthur New Testament Commentary: John 1–11* (Chicago, IL: Moody Publishers, 2006), 140.

EXPERIENCING JESUS THROUGH THE EYES OF THE SAMARITAN WOMAN

what Jesus says in verse 34: "Jesus said to them, 'my food is to do the will of him who sent me and to accomplish his work.'" Jesus' food was to do the work the Father sent Him to do, and that was to break in and spread the kingdom of God from Jerusalem to the ends of the world. Jesus knew His mission, and He was very intentional in His mission.

As Christians, we need to be very intentional as we seek to live on mission and engage with the world with the good news of the gospel. If we want to reach out to communities, our country, and the nations with the gospel of Jesus Christ, then we have to be intentional. Before we discuss different ways Christians can be intentional with gospel engagement, how does intentionality look and feel for those we are trying to engage? How did Jesus intentionality affect the Samaritan woman? I truly do not believe the woman knew how intentional Jesus was when He "had to pass through Samaria," but as Jesus engaged with her, I do believe she was affected. Remember, this woman was isolated and excommunicated from the other women in her village, so imagine how she felt when Jesus engaged with her.

Verse 7 tells us how when the woman came to the well, Jesus engaged her by asking her for a drink. In verse 9, we see the shock she experiences as Jesus engages her. She stated, "How is it that you, a Jew, ask for a drink for me, a woman of Samaria?" First, she was startled because a man approached her. In this culture, men did not engage with women, and women did not engage with men. I have been on some mission trips to Muslim countries and the first thing they teach you is that the men need only to engage the men, and women need only to engage women. Second, a Jew would have never engaged a Samaritan. Remember, the Jews and Samaritans hated each other, so this this would never happen. The Jews would avoid dealing with a Samaritan at whatever cost. For Jesus to engage this woman, this was going completely against the culture and this would have never happened. Just imagine how greatly this probably affected her because remember no one in her own village would engage her, and now there is this Jewish man engaging her with a friendly conversation. I personally believe one of the reasons this woman was open to talking with Jesus and eventually was open to the gospel was because of Jesus intentionality with engaging her. Sam Greer stated, "By Jesus' speaking to her He was breaking down cultural, racial, social, religious, gender and generational barriers."[23] Tony Evans stated, "One of the greatest evangelistic outreaches occurred simply because Jesus took the time to engage and connect with another person from another background than His own."[24]

As Christians, as we go out and engage the world, we must be very intentional, and we must be ready to get out of our comfort zone and engage people by spending time with them, serving them, and praying for them in the hopes of the opportunity to share the gospel with them. When we do this, I believe this will make a great impact in people's lives and open their hearts and minds to the gospel. The problem that I see in our country is that we are being comforted to death. We can shop online, go to the doctor online, almost do anything without ever leaving the comfort of our homes. We are becoming more and more isolated from each other, and if we are isolated from each other, how can we engage with people, build a relationship with them, and share the gospel with them? In the book *Bowling Alone*, the author basically reveals how over the past fifty or so years our society has become increasingly disconnected from family, friends, neighbors, and social structures.[25] More and more people are isolating from community life. As Christians, we must resist the urge to stay in our comfortable lives by staying within the walls of our home or within the walls of our church, and we must get out of comfortability and get outside the walls of our home and the walls of our church and engage our communities with the gospel of Jesus. I know when I get home all I really want to do is to eat dinner with my family, sit down with my family, and watch TV. There is nothing wrong with this, but then I look outside, and I see lots of people out in our neighborhood and I think to myself I really do not want to, but to live with intentionality means I must do what I do not want to do and get out into my neighborhood and meet my neighbors to

---

[23] Sam Greer, *The Gospel Conversationalist* (Bloomington: IN, Zondervan, 2018), 57.
[24] Tony Evans, *Oneness Embraced: Reconciliation, The Kingdom, and How We are Stronger Together* (Chicago, IL: Moody Publishers, 2011), 67.
[25] Robert Putnam, *Bowling Alone* (New York, NY: Simon & Schuster, 2000).

build relationships with them in the hopes of sharing the gospel with them. If we are going to reach our neighborhoods and our community with the gospel, then we must be intentional. This may mean actually going to the grocery store or actually going to the doctor's office or actually going to places in our communities and meet people. You may be reading this and thinking this is scary, and this is uncomfortable, and yes, it is, but again, if we truly want to fulfill the Great Commission and engage the world with the gospel, then we will have to get out of our comfort zone and go where people are in order to build relationships with them in order to serve them, show them, and proclaim to them the gospel of Jesus Christ.

This is what we see happening with the early followers of Jesus. In Acts 8:4, it says, "They preached the word wherever they went." These believers were basically proclaiming the gospel of Jesus wherever they went: in their homes, in the synagogue, in the marketplace, and in their workplace. In the book *Evangelism in the Early Church*, Michael Green stated,

> The early church saw themselves as evangelists just as much as the apostles. Their spreading of the gospel, must often have been not formal preaching, but the informal chattering to friends and chance acquaintances, in homes, on walks, and around market stalls. They went everywhere gossiping the gospel; they did it naturally, enthusiastically, and with the conviction of those who are not paid to say that sort of thing. Consequently, they were taken seriously; and the movement spread, notably among the lower class.[26]

---

[26] Michael Green, *Evangelism in the Early Church,* rev. ed. (Grand Rapids, MI: Eerdmans, 2003), 246.

Larry Sharp stated, "The mission of God suggests that everyone should live out God's mission in every aspect of life-all the time, and in every way and in every place."[27]

The good news is that even though it is uncomfortable and scary, we do not have to do alone. In fact, we cannot do it alone, but as we go out, we go out with God's presence and His power. In Acts 1:8, Jesus stated, "But you will receive power when the Holy Spirit has come upon you, and you will be my witnesses in Jerusalem, in all Judea, Samaria and to the ends of the earth."

Jesus was about to leave the earth and go to be with the Father, but before He left, He told the disciples that He would send the Holy Spirit, and when the Spirit comes, they would then go and be His witnesses all over the world. Jesus knew that if He would have sent them out for His mission alone, they would have failed miserably. This is why in Acts 1:4, He told them to go back to Jerusalem and wait until the Holy Spirit comes and then they would go and be His witnesses. Jesus did not send them alone. He sent them out with His presence and His power through the Holy Spirit. Jesus sent His apostles out with the Spirit, and He sends His church out with the same Spirit so as we go out to engage the world we go out with the same Spirit who raised Jesus from the dead, the same Spirit who He sent with His disciples.

We have the same presence and the same power because we have the Holy Spirit who indwells within us, and do you know what the Spirit wants to do? He wants to proclaim the gospel. Every time in the book of Acts when you see the disciples being filled with the Spirit, the next thing you see them do is to proclaim the gospel. In Acts chapter 2, Peter is filled with the Spirit, and he then proclaims the gospel. Acts 4:8 says Peter is filled with the Spirt, and then he proclaims the gospel. In Acts 4:31, it says the disciples were all filled with the Sprit and they "continued to speak the word of God with boldness."

---

[27] Larry Sharp, *Missions Disrupted* (Peabody, MA: Hendrickson Publishing, 2022), 23.

EXPERIENCING JESUS THROUGH THE EYES OF THE SAMARITAN WOMAN

As Jesus sends us out, He sends us out with His presence and His power through the Holy Spirit. In the hearts of the civil rights movement, Martin Luther King Jr. found himself at a crossroad. He could walk away from the effort or keep going. He was threatened, attacked, and begged by his parents to walk away; but he was drawn to this movement by something much bigger, God. One night, as he could not sleep, he sat there, scared and weak, and he called out to God. He said,

> Lord, I'm down here trying to do what's right. But Lord, I must confess that I am weak. I am faltering. I am losing my courage. And it seemed at that moment I could hear an inner voice saying to me. "Martin Luther, stand up for righteousness. Stand up for justice, stand up for the truth. And lo, I will be with you, even until the end of the world."[28]

Martin Luther King Jr. found new strength and courage because he was reminded why he was doing what he was doing. This is what God was calling him to do. To fight for righteousness and to fight for justice. He knew it would not be easy, but he knew God would be with him. As Christians, we must be confident that as we go out and engage the world, we go out with God's presence and His power. We know it will not be easy, but we can know God will be with us. One important truth we must also understand is how we experience the presence and power of Jesus. Some people think to themselves whenever God gives me this unbelievable power or courage to go and do what he is calling me to do, then I will go and do it, but not until Then." The problem is that this is not how God normally works. God can do whatever He wants, but again, He normally does not work this way.

---

[28] David Garrow, *Bearing The Cross* (New York, NY: Harper Collins Publishers, 1986), 58.

So how does He work? God's presence and power is felt the moment we act out in faith. Let me give you an example. In the movie *Indiana Jones and the Holy Grail*, there is a scene where Indiana must pass over this bridge to get to the Holy Grail and save his father. The problem is that the bridge is invisible. You cannot see the bridge; you must believe it exist. You must have faith. As Indiana approaches the bridge, he had to have faith the bridge was there, and then he had to act out his faith by taking a step onto the bridge. The moment Indiana took the step of faith, that is the moment when he was able to see the bridge, but not a moment before.

This is how God's presence and power is felt. His presence and power are there, but we must have faith, and we must act on that faith and take a step, and the moment we take that step of faith, is the moment when we feel His presence and power. So the moment we take the step of faith and engage the world with the gospel, that is the moment when we will feel and experience His presence and power and not a moment sooner. As we engage the world, have faith and take the step of faith, knowing that God is with us, and we have His power.

Not only does Jesus send us out with His presence and His power, but more good news is that as we go out, we cannot be stopped because the gospel cannot be stopped because God cannot be stopped. In Matthew chapter 16, Jesus tells us that He will build His church and the gates of hell shall not prevail. A gate is a defense weapon. The gospel is the offense and Jesus tells us the defense cannot stop us. Think about a football game. The offense runs the play and the defense has to stop them, but here Jesus says the defense cannot stop this offense. How encouraging is this!

I was watching a football game and Wisconsin, coached by Brett Bielema, blew out their opponent. At the end of the game, the media was blasting Coach Bielema because in their minds, he had run up the scoreboard. Coach Bielema reminded them his job as a coach is to score touchdowns and it is the other team's job to stop them. No matter if you agree or disagree with him, he has a good point. This is the beauty of the gospel. We are the offense, and the defense cannot stop us.

EXPERIENCING JESUS THROUGH THE EYES OF THE SAMARITAN WOMAN

I think one of the problems in the church today is we have lost our position. Most of us think or at least act like we are the spectators. They think the Great Commission is for only a special group of Christians or only for pastors and church leaders who get paid to do ministry. Elton Trueblood, in his book *The Company of the Committed*, stated, "The call to witness is a call which men can answer affirmatively or negatively, but one who answers it negatively, however kind and pious he may be, is not in the company of Jesus."[29] In the book *Missions Disrupted*, Larry Sharp states how he believes there are lots of pews in churches today where the people in them do not see themselves as beneficial or having a purpose in missions because they have felt this responsibility was only for professional ministers and missionaries. He goes on to say that he was talking with a believer one morning and this man told him, "I don't see that I have anything to offer the world of missions."[30]

Dustin Willis and Aaron Coe state in *Life on Mission*,

> Many people believe that mission and ministry are carried out by a select few professional clergy or an elite number of mission agencies and non profit organizations. But the reality: God's mission was given to every member of His church. We are called to be everyday missionaries. Everyday missionaries are those who practice life on mission where God has placed them, whether that be at the office complex, a developing country, or a college campus. It is incumbent on every believer to have an 'all hands on deck' mentality in order for the mission to reach its fullest potential.[31]

---

[29] Elton Trueblood, *The Company of the Committed* (HarperCollins, 1979), 49.
[30] Larry Sharp, *Missions Disrupted: From Professional Missionaries to Missional Professionals* (Peabody, MA: Hendrickson Publishers, 2022), 33.
[31] Dustin Willis & Aaron Coe, *Life on Mission: Joining the Everyday Mission of God* (Chicago, IL: Moody Publishers, 2014), 26.

Think about this: what if you were watching a football game and the team huddled up, the quarterback called the play, the huddle broke, and the entire team ran into the stands? You would probably think these players are crazy. Their job is not to watch the play, their job is to do what? Run the play.

In Matthew 28, Jesus has given us the play, and He is giving us all we need, so what are we to do? We are to run the play! The truth is God does not have a Great Commission Navy SEAL team who He sends out to fulfill the Great Commission. All believers are called to the Great Commission. The moment you became a Christian was the moment God commanded you to now go and intentionally share the good news of the gospel with the world. The good news is that as we go out and spread the gospel, we cannot be stopped. In 1791, on John Wesley's deathbed, his last letter he ever wrote was to William Wilberforce, who was fighting to abolish the slave trade. Listen to what Wesley says to Wilberforce:

> Dear sir: unless the divine power has raised you up to be as "Athanasius against the world," I see not how you can go through your glorious enterprise in opposing that unpleasant villainy… Unless God has raised you up for this very thing, you will be worn out by the opposition of men and devils. But if God be for you, who can be against you?… Go on in the name of God and in the power of his might, till even American slavery shall vanish away before it.[32]

John Wesley is telling Wilberforce if God is not in this you have no chance, but if God is in this keep going and do not stop because you cannot be stopped because God cannot be stopped. The truth is that as we go and engage the world, it will not be easy, but we can

---

[32] Letter from Wesley to Wilberforce on February 24, 1791, https://medium.com/@rickhogaboam/john-wesleys-final-letter-to-william-wilberforce-slavery-and-the-sanctity-of-life-571538291c16.

have the promise and the confidence that God not only will be with us, but we cannot be stopped because the gospel cannot be stopped, so be encouraged to keep going.

So as we go out with God's presence and His power and we know the gospel cannot be stopped, how do we live our life with intentionality? In the book *Total Church*, Tim Chester and Steve Timmis stated, "Gospel ministry is ordinary people doing ordinary thing with gospel intention."[33] What are ordinary things? Ordinary things are whatever we do in our normal lives. This means that as I go to work, I go with gospel intention, as I go out into my community I go out with gospel intention, and as I go out and play sports, I play sports with gospel intention. Chester and Timmis stated, "Whether it is helping a friend, working at the office, or going to the movies, there is a commitment to building relationships, modeling the Christian faith, and talking about the gospel as a natural part of conversation."[34] As we go out and live in this world and do our ordinary activities, we must learn to live and be committed to live with gospel intention. Martin Luther would say lots of Christians try to wear two hats. One hat is their sacred hat they wear on Sundays, but as soon as Sunday is over, they take off their sacred and put on their secular hat, and they wear this hat from Monday through Saturday. The truth is that Christians only have one hat, and we must wear that hat every day. As God's people, we are always on mission. When we go to work, we are on mission; when we go out into the community, we are always on mission; and when we go to the ballfield, we are always on mission. So how do we practically do this?

At Work

When it comes to living with gospel intentionality, how can we do this at the workplace? The most important thing to remember is that as a follower of Christ, we are always representing Christ. In

---

[33] Tim Chester and Steve Timmis, *Total Church* (Wheaton, IL: Crossway, 2008), 63.
[34] Ibid.

his book *Every Square Inch*, Bruce Ashford stated, "Our job opportunities to witness about Christ precisely by backing up our words with actions. Not only do we let people know verbally that Christ is Lord, but we also do our work in a way that is shaped by Christ and His Word."[35] How does a Christian represent Christ honorably and reflect the gospel at work? In order to be a witness to Christ at work, we must always be on time, work hard and always have a good attitude. How do you think it would look if you were always late, lazy, and always complained? It would not only bring dishonor to God, but it would also distort our gospel message.

We must always be respectful to our bosses and to other employees. Do not be involved in gossip. Get to know other employees, take them to lunch, and show them you truly do care about them. As Christians, we must be different from the world, and so if we are different from the other employees in a good way, people will wonder why we are different, and this gives us opportunities to share with others why we are different. We can share we are different because we are followers of Jesus in the hopes that they will want to know more about Jesus.

We do not have to be in people's faces with the gospel or try to force the Bible and the gospel down their throats, but we can be open about our faith and share our lives with others. When I was working at Powerade, I was never shy about my faith. I was always open about my faith. One time I was getting ready to go on a mission trip, and I told all my clients where I was going and what I was doing. When I got back, one of my clients asked me to sit down with him and tell him more about my trip. We literally spent an hour in his office talking, not about work-related items, but about my mission trip and me going to tell them about Jesus.

Again, we do not have to shove the Bible down people's throats, but we can be open about our faith and what all God has done in our lives. On Mondays, while people were telling what they did for the weekend, I would tell people about what I learned in church or

---

[35] Bruce Riley Ashford, *Every Square Inch: An Introduction to Cultural Engagement for Christians* (Bellingham, WA: Lexham Press, 2015).

about my mission trip or about my serving opportunity I had over the weekend. The key to living on mission in the workplace is to be open about your faith, let people know where you stand and be different. When we live this way in our workplace, trust me, it gets noticed. If you are the first one to work, the hardest worker and always have a positive attitude people will notice, and they will want to know why you are the way you are and then this opens the door for a gospel conversation.

Before we move on, I must share a painful truth when it comes to the workplace. There may come a time where you are asked to do something or stand with something that goes against your biblical convictions. If this day, we must not let this stand in the way of our witness to the truth, and we may have to walk away from that job. I know this is not easy to hear, but I believe it is the truth. I was in Cuba on a mission trip one year, and while I was gone, our company started talking about promoting pride month within our athletic teams, which means I would have had to promote this, which in my biblical convictions I could not. As I was in Cuba, I started to pray, and I remember telling my family that my time with this company may be coming to an end. It would not have been easy, but it would be the right thing to do, and so I was prepared to walk away. The good news was that we did not have to do this, so I did not have to walk way, but I was prepared to if I would have had to. If you have been in this situation, or if you find yourself in this situation, please know that you can trust God to provide, and the truth is we must never let anything stand in the way of our witness to the gospel, even a great job.

A newer concept to live on mission in the workplace is called Business as Mission (BAM). Larry Sharp, in his book *Mission Disrupted*, says this concept came around in the early nineties.[36] Business as Mission is Christians leveraging the marketplace to live on mission and fulfill the Great Commission. Sharp stated, "It is living out the commands of Jesus in the workplace: to love our neigh-

---

[36] Larry Sharp, *Missions Disrupted: From Professional Missionaries to Missional Professionals* (Peabody, MA: Hendrickson Publishers, 2022).

bor and make disciples so individuals and communities are transformed—spiritually, economically, and socially—for the greater glory of God and the establishment of his church."[37] Christians utilizing their work or their personal business can get access and opportunities that a missionary or someone in full-time ministry will never be able to. JD Greear stated, "Christians in the marketplace today are able to gain access more easily to strategic, unreached places. Globalization, great advancements in technology, and urbanization have given the business community nearly universal access."[38]

Business as Mission has many advantages, both economical and spiritual. BAMs will create jobs, and be profitable, which has a great impact economically. BAMs also is a good steward of God's creation. As Christians, we are to care for God's creation (Genesis 1:15). BAM also fulfills the Great Commission by making disciples. Sharp stated, in summary,

> A kingdom business has a quadruple bottom line that includes profit because this is what sustains an authentic economic life; it includes job creation because this helps fulfill the Great Commandment to love our neighbor; and it includes the making of disciples of Jesus so we can obey the Great Commission while caring for the creation in every respect.[39]

Patrick Tsague of the Nehemiah Project stated,

> Simply put, a Kingdom business is God's business, managed God's way, by God's steward, for God's purposes in the world. The business operations must be managed by the guidelines of

---

[37] Ibid., 61.
[38] J. D. Greear, "The Next Wave of Missions," *J.D. Greear Ministries*, December 2, 2011, http://jdgreear.com/blog/the-next-wave-of-missions/.
[39] Larry Sharp, *Missions Disrupted: From Professional Missionaries to Missional Professionals* (Peabody, MA: Hendrickson Publishers, 2022), 68.

the King which are found in the Bible. Moreover, the products and services must be approved by the King; thus, there should be no sin products. The business must be where we demonstrate our salt and light to a dark and dying world. And of course, it must be profitable since the King is concerned about the proper stewardship of His resources. However, the profit is not for us, the operators of a Kingdom business, but for the King, the owner of the business, so we must use the profits as He directs.[40]

In Your Neighborhood

One of the easiest ways to live on mission in your neighborhood is to do routine walks through your neighborhood and prayer walk. Pray for each individual house. Take walks in your neighborhood and try to meet your neighbors. Be a good neighbor. Do not gossip about your neighbors. Find ways to love on and serve your neighbors. Try to help them with their yard work. During bad storms and emergencies, check on your neighbors. I know one year we had a really bad snowstorm. Yes, I did say we actually had a bad snowstorm in Alabama. It does happen. One thing my wife and I did during the storm was we went around and checked on all our neighbors and offered to help them with any needs they may have. When you know they are going out of town offer to babysit their pets, check on their house, grab their mail while they are gone. Do whatever you can to be a good neighbor when they are not in town.

When you see needs within your neighborhood, try to help. One day during COVID lockdown, my wife and I were walking through our neighborhood, prayer walking and trying to check on neighbors when we saw a man fall down into his front yard. We stopped and helped him get up, and then we tried to knock on the

---

[40] Patrick Tsague, "What Is a Kingdom Business?" *Regent University Center for Entrepreneurship*, https://regententrepreneur.org/what-is-kingdom-business/.

door to see if his wife would come outside and help get him in the house, but she must have been afraid and would not open the door so we had to prop him up on his truck bed and left, hoping she would eventually come out and get him. It does not always work out the way you hope, but you still try.

After work and on weekends, hang out on the front porch or in the yard and try to meet people as they pass by. I went to a comedy show one time, and the comedian said the problem in the world today is that families have quit hanging out on front porches and, instead, have started to hang out on the back deck. He then says, "If Opie Taylor from *The Andy Griffin Show* would have had a deck, he would have been on drugs." There is nothing wrong with hanging out on the back deck, but we may need to sometimes hang out in the front yard or on the front porch in order to try to engage with our neighbors.

One of the best ways to live on mission with your neighbors is to invite them over for dinner. Francis Schaeffer and his daughter created an environment in their home, which allowed unbelievers to share meals with them, to live life together, to experience Christian love, and to be able to ask questions about Christianity. We will go into this in more depth in chapter 5. Host a game or movie night for your neighborhood. Invite your neighbors to church. Start a Bible study and invite your neighbors. During the holidays, take snacks, food, and small gifts to your neighbors. Host an Easter egg hunt for your neighborhood. During sporting events, do a cookout and invite your neighbors.

Before we move on to the next section, let's address being intentional cross-culturally in your neighborhood. The truth is that God is sending the nations to us. If you are like me, you probably have neighbors who may not look like you, so how can you engage them intentionally? Imagine how you would feel if you moved to a new country and to a different culture. You probably would feel scared, and so one easy way is to welcome them to your neighborhood with some type of gift. Invite them to dinner. Leviticus 19:34 states, "You shall treat the stranger who sojourns with you as the native among you, and you shall love him as yourself, for you were strangers in the land of Egypt: I am the Lord your God."

Dustin Willis and Brandon Clements in the book *The Simplest Way to Change the World* stated, "Regardless of our political stances on immigration, as Christians, we have no excuse for neglecting to welcome strangers and foreigners around us. We were once strangers who needed to be included and welcomed. In light of that knowledge, we must do the same for others."[41] You can volunteer to help them get settled into our culture. My church partnered with a church plant in Clarkston, Georgia, who was planting a church for refugees. Clarkston, Georgia, is one of the largest United Nations refugee resettlements in the country. I learned from the pastor that the UN gives them ninety days of support once they enter the country. Can you imagine moving to another country and only getting help for ninety days? I cannot imagine moving to another state and only getting ninety days of support. How great would it be and how much of an impact would it make if you committed to helping them get settled?

The key to living on mission in your neighborhood is to make the time to be available. I said this already, but the one thing I want to do at night after work and on weekends is to just lie around the house and spend time with my family and read books, but if I want to live on mission, then I must be willing to come out of my comfort zone and get out into my neighborhood, meet my neighbors, and build intentional relationships with them in the hopes of being a witness to Jesus to them. Williams and College stated,

> It takes only your willingness to open your home and life to others. Many Christians believe that in order to be part of God's mission, they have to do something drastic. But the reality is you can be an integral part of His mission from

---

[41] Dustin Williams and Brandon College, *The Simplest Way to Change the World: Biblical Hospitality as a Way of Life* (Chicago, IL: Moody Publishers, 2017), 140–141.

right where you are, without leaving the home you sleep in each night.[42]

In the Community

When it comes to intentional living on mission in the community, there are numerous opportunities. Get involved in nonprofit organizations that serve the community. In my community, there is a local nonprofit agency that serves the community by providing food, clothing, household items, baby items, and many other items. My family and I have served with this ministry many times. Get involved in sports activities. Sign your children up to play community or school sports, volunteer at local sporting events, or volunteer to coach your children's teams. Getting involved in local sports and sporting events is a great way to meet people with the hopes of building relationships that can lead to gospel conversations.

Take an active involvement in local politics and government. Serve on a local school board, serve at your children's school(s), or offer to serve a need within a local school. One of the things my wife and I do is to contact our son's school and teachers and see how we can meet any needs. This may mean being a chaperone, supplying supplies and snacks for the teachers, and offering to come and read to the students. Be active in your children's school activities. Attend any activities, such as awards, pep rallies, sporting events, and/or have school lunch with your children. These are all good ways to meet school administrators, teachers, students, and students' parents with the hope of building relationships and being a gospel witness.

Get out of the house and visit local places routinely. Get out of the house one day and work at a local coffee shop or another local hangout. Joining a gym is a great way to meet people and build relationships. In my earlier story, this is how I met my friend at the gym, and we went from meeting each other to meeting up every day to work out together.

---

[42] Dustin Williams and Brandon College, *The Simplest Way to Change the World: Biblical Hospitality as a Way of Life* (Chicago, IL: Moody Publishers, 2017), 19.

EXPERIENCING JESUS THROUGH THE EYES OF THE SAMARITAN WOMAN

Instead of always trying new coffee shops and restaurants, try going to the same one or ones to get to know the servers and other people. Before you eat, tell your server how you are about to pray for the meal and ask them if there is anything you can pray for them. I heard a pastor state that he and his family were out to dinner one evening, and as they were about to eat, he asked the server if there were anything he could pray for her. He then stated before they left the server pulled him aside and told him her story about her son who was in jail for drugs and asked if he would pray for her and her son. The pastor said he then shared the gospel with her right there in the restaurant. During the COVID lockdown, when the restaurants were starting to open back up, our church identified several restaurants in the area, and we encouraged church members to go these restaurants and bless them by purchasing food and then to give them a prayer card stating Valleydale Church is praying for you. Our church members loved this idea.

Another good opportunity is going to the same hairstylist or barber shop. This will give you the opportunity to get to know them, build a relationship with them with the hopes of sharing the gospel with them. I heard a pastor say that no matter where he has lived, he has always went to the same barber, and because of this, he has been able to share the gospel with all of them because he has built a relationship with them, which has led to having gospel conversations.

One of my favorite things my wife and I did was every Friday we went to the same pizza place and we sit at the bar (not to drink), and over time, we met all the bartenders and servers, got to know them, and then started learning more about them personally. This led to us learning about their families, their situations, and any problems they were having or struggling with. A couple of bartenders started feeling comfortable enough with us to share prayer request prayer requests. Even to this day, some of them, even though they have left that restaurant, still contact us for prayer and help. The truth about going to the same places and getting to know the people is that you can continue to go back and continue any conversations you may have had. If they have been sick, you can follow up with them the next time they are in there. No matter what they are going through, you can always follow up with them the next time you are in there. If you do this, please make sure you are a good customer and a good tipper. It does not do you very well if you are trying to build a relationship with the servers in the hopes of leading to a gospel conversation with them and then turn around are not a good customer or are not a good tipper. This will kill any opportunity you have.

Look for opportunities for personal evangelism at parks, gym, pool, or any other local community hangouts. Go where people hang out and look for opportunities for personal evangelism. In the book *The Great Good Place* by Ray Oldenburg, he describes what he calls "third place."[43] "Third place" are public places where people hang out, such as gyms, coffeeshops, barbershops, hair salons, or parks. Another way to be intentional about evangelism is to engage in door-to-door evangelism. I know this seems terrifying, but I have been involved in this a few times, and one thing I have learned is it is not as bad as you think. Before you go out, you imagine all these horrible thoughts in your mind of how people are going to hate you and do not want anything to do with you and will not even open the doors to you. Do not get me wrong, some houses that you visit will pretty quickly tell you they are not interested, but in my experience, far more people will actually sit and have a conversation with you. Most people I have knocked on their door have been very courteous and respectable even if they do not believe what you believe. Now I know I live in the Bible belt, but all the fears I have built up in my head are nothing compared to my actual experience as I have went out. Give it a try some time; you might just be surprised.

Government

> Let every person be subject to the governing authorities. For there is no authority except from God, and those that exist have been instituted

---

[43] Ray Oldenburg, *The Great Good Place: Cafes, Coffee Shops, Bookstores, Bars, Hair Salons, and Other Hangouts at the Heart of a Community* (Philadelphia, PA: Da Capo, 1999), 14.

by God. Therefore whoever resists the authorities resists what God has appointed, and those who resist will incur judgment. for rulers are not a terror to good conduct, but to bad. Would you have no fear of the one who is in authority? Then do what is good, and you will receive his approval, for he is God's servant for your good. But if you do wrong, be afraid, for he does not bear the sword in vain. For he is the servant of God, and avenger who carries out God's wrath on the wrongdoer. Therefore one must be in subjection, not only to avoid God's wrath but also for the sake of conscience. For because of this you also pay taxes for the authorities are ministers of God, attending to this very thing. Pay to all what is owed to them; taxes to whom taxes are owed, revenue to whom revenue is owed, respect to whom respect is owed, honor to whom honor is owed. (Romans 13:1–7)

Be subject for the Lord's sake to every human institution, whether it be to the emperor as supreme, or to governors as sent by him to punish those who do good. For this is the will of God, that by doing good you should put to silence the ignorance of foolish people. Live as people who are free, not using your freedom as a cover-up for evil, but living as servants of God. Honor everyone. Love the brotherhood. Fear God. Honor the emperor. (1 Peter 2:13–17)

Paul and Peter tell us that Christians are to respect our governing authorities. First, because God has established these governments. Second, because these governments are to promote good in human flourishing and to punish evil. Third, to be a witness. In order for Christians to live missionally toward the government they are to respect the government. We are to be the best citizens. We are to uphold the laws. We are to promote peace. We are to do good. Patrick Schreiner, in his book *Political Gospel*, stated,

> This is not ultimately our home, we are just passing through, but in the meantime, we are not against the world but for it. We seek to bless the nations amid our sojourning. The exile assembly is given some surprising advice. As a body politic, we are to conduct ourselves honorably among the Gentiles.[44]

He goes on to say,

> We are to act virtuously, despite the antagonism. As visitors here on earth, we are to be good guests. Insofar as it relies upon us, we live quiet lives, avoid negative stereotypes, and seek to do good to all people. We are to live among our neighbors (not separate from them), but in an upright way (avoiding evil). It is lifestyle evangelism.[45]

Christians are to be peaceful, loving, and we are to seek the good of others. In 1 Thessalonians 4:9–12, Paul tells Christians to live quiet lives, mind your own affairs, and work. Schreiner stated, "Paul says heavenly citizens fly under the radar. He wants us to be normal Joes and Janes who go to work, come home to our family, serve the city, and love our neighbors."[46]

> Thus says the Lord of hosts, the God of Israel, to all the exiles whom I have sent into exile

---

[44] Patrick Schreiner, *Political Gospel: Public Witness in a Politically Crazy World* (Brentwood, TN: B&H Publishing, 2023), 114.
[45] Ibid.
[46] Patrick Schreiner, *Political Gospel: Public Witness in a Politically Crazy World* (Brentwood, TN: B&H Publishing, 2023), 176.

> from Jerusalem to Babylon: Build houses and live in them; plant gardens and eat their produce. Take wives and have sons and daughters; take wives for your sons, and give your daughters in marriage, that they may bear sons and daughters; multiply there, and do not decrease. But seek the welfare of the city where I have sent you into exile, and pray to the Lord on its behalf, for in its welfare you will find your welfare. (Jeremiah 29:4–7)

Christians should be the first to seek the good of the city. We should be the first to respect our government. We should pray for them, and we should pray and push toward flourishing of our nations. We should be active citizens. We should not flee or retreat from the public arena, but we are to be in the public arena, and most importantly, we are to be a witness to the gospel of Jesus Christ while we continue to live in the public sphere. Christians should take an active role in serving governmental agencies. My church currently works with and serves with our local police department and our local Department of Human Resources for foster ministry opportunities. I personally serve on the board of a county free medical clinic. The key is for Christians is to find intentional ways to serve and support our government agencies and officials.

Church

What are some way you can live missionally within the local church. Let me tell you my story. After college, I moved to Birmingham, Alabama, where I eventually met my wife. My wife and I were neither, at the time, connected to a local church. One day, we decided to find a local church, and looked in the phone book and found the closest church, which was Valleydale Church. My wife and I eventually joined the church, which we are still members of today, but for a number of years, we just showed up for worship service and that was about it. One year, we decided to both read the Bible in a year, and this was the beginning of our journey that we are still on. God started working in our lives, and we both started getting involved in the church. I was working at Powerade at the time, and I started reading the book *Radical* by David Platt. God really used this book to radically change my life, no pun intended.

I remember I was on a trip when I finished the book. I called my wife and told her that when I got back, things needed to change. At this time, I had never been on a mission trip and really did not know much about missions. I called the current missions pastor and set up a meeting with him. When I met with him, I told him I knew nothing about missions and had never been on a mission trip, but God was calling me to missions in some capacity, which at the time, I had no clue in what way. At that moment, the missions pastor got me involved with missions, which I have been heavily involved in since, and it is even funny how a number of years later, I would become the mission pastor at Valleydale Church. If you are wondering if God has a sense of humor, the answer is yes, He does.

I say all this to say, if you want to truly live on mission in your local church, just go and set up a meeting with the missions team, and I am sure they will have you on as many missions trips as you want to go on. If you truly want to live missionally in your local church, seriously, go on a mission trip. Take your family on a short-term trip. You can also consider going on a midterm mission trip, or maybe, just maybe, God will call you to go long term. I know you may be saying at this moment, this will never happen. Just keep in mind, I had never been on a mission trip, and after my first trip, it was not too many years later that God called me to the ministry. So do not say He will not. Trust me!

You can serve your local community through your church. Go and talk to your church about serving at one of their local ministry partners. If you are involved in a small group, consider planning a serving opportunity with your small group or consider going on a mission trip with your small group. One of the things we are trying to do at Valleydale is to get our small groups to adopt something within the community like a local school or a local neighborhood and build a ministry around whatever this may be. The bottom line is if you truly want to live missionally within your church, it is not hard at all. You can just grab your small group or grab some friends or just grab your family and find a way to serve your community or go on a mission trip together. If you do not feel comfortable doing this on your own, just go and talk to your missions staff, and I am sure they will help you out. I know if you came and talked to me, I would be very happy and glad to help you. Another way to live on mission within your church is just by inviting nonbelievers to your church. As I write this, I am in San Diego hanging out with some church planters, and one of the planters took us around his community, he gave everyone he came into contact with an invite card to his church. Go and talk to your church and see if they have any church invite cards; if not, ask them if they would potentially make some so that you and other church members can go out into the community, your neighborhoods, and your workplace and give out these cards and invite people to church.

Conclusion

When it comes to living with intentionality, no matter if it is at work, in your neighborhood, in the community, in the government, or in your local church, the key is to be visible and to be available. Be willing to get out of your comfort zone, out of your private lives, and get out into the public. Be encouraged: it will take time, sacrifice, and hard work; but over time, God will give you opportunities to meet people, build relationships, and have gospel conversations. We just have to be willing and available to do what God is calling us to do, and that is to live our lives with gospel intention. We must also be obedient when God gives us opportunities to meet people, build relationships, and share the gospel. Remember, God is always with you, and He empowers us through the Holy Spirit. Willis and Coe stated, "When we combine our natural rhythms or passions with the gospel and use them to build relationships, powerful things happen. Our passions or placement (where we live, where we go) can help us identify opportunities for sharing the gospel."[47]

---

[47] Dustin Willis & Aaron Coe, *Life on Mission: Joining the Everyday Mission of God* (Chicago, IL: Moody Publishers, 2014), 112.

3

Jesus Listened

I will bless the Lord at all times; his praise shall continually be in my mouth. My soul makes its boast in the Lord; let the humble hear and be glad. Oh, magnify the Lord with me, and let us exalt his name together! I sought the Lord, and he answered me and delivered me from all my fears. Those who look to him are radiant, and their faces shall never be ashamed. This poor man cried, and the Lord heard him and saved him out of all his troubles. The angel of the Lord encamps around those who fear him, and delivers them. Oh, taste and see that the Lord is good! Blessed is the man who takes refuge in him! Oh, fear the Lord, you his saints, for those who fear him have no lack! The young lions suffer want and hunger; but those who seek the Lord lack no good thing. Come, O children, listen to me; I will teach you the fear of the Lord. What man is there who desires life and loves many days, that he may see good? Keep your tongue from evil and your lips from speaking deceit. Turn away from evil and do good; seek peace and pursue it. The eyes of the Lord are toward the righteous and

> his ears toward their cry. The face of the Lord is against those who do evil, to cut off the memory of them from the earth. When the righteous cry for help, the Lord hears and delivers them out of all their troubles. The Lord is near to the brokenhearted and saves the crushed in spirit. Many are the afflictions of the righteous, but the Lord delivers him out of them all. He keeps all his bones; not one of them is broken. Affliction will slay the wicked, and those who hate the righteous will be condemned. The Lord redeems the life of his servants; none of those who take refuge in him will be condemned. (Psalm 34:1–22)

My son was born with Down syndrome, and we learned pretty quickly after he was born that he had trouble with his hearing. Because of his hearing trouble, my wife and I decided to get him cochlear implants. Cochlear implant is a small, complex electronic device that provides a sense of sound to a person who has limited hearing. So when it comes to hearing, trust me, I know how important it is. But here is a truth that I have learned from experience: there is a difference between hearing and listening. Just because we can hear does not mean we are listening. I am guilty of this all the time with my wife. She will be talking to me and I can hear her, but she quickly learns that I am not always listening.

James 1:19 states, "Know this, my beloved brothers: let every person be quick to hear, slow to speak, slow to anger." I believe James knows we are fast talkers, but we are not good at listening. Have you ever heard the phrase that there is a reason God gave us two ears and one mouth? The truth is that we are very fast at speaking and giving our thoughts, but we are very poor at listening. Let me prove it to you. How many of you have ever had a conversation where a friend, family member, coworker is sharing a problem with you, and while they are sharing this problem with you, you have quickly made an assessment and have already come up with a solution, and they are still presenting the problem to you? Is this you?

What about this: have you ever been in a group discussion, and someone is talking or giving their idea and you are no longer listening, but are just waiting for them to finish so you can speak and give your thoughts? Is this you? I personally am guilty of both of these. The truth is that we all find ourselves hearing someone, but really not listening and when it comes to living on mission and engaging people we must learn to truly listen to them. As Jesus engaged with the Samaritan woman, we see Jesus intently listened to her.

> So he came to a town of Samaria called Sychar, near the field that Jacob had given to his son Joseph. Jacob's well was there; so Jesus, wearied as he was from his journey, was sitting beside the well. It was about the sixth hour. A woman from Samaria came to draw water. Jesus said to her, "Give me a drink." (For his disciples had gone away into the city to buy food.) The Samaritan woman said to him, "How is it that you, a Jew, ask for a drink from me, a woman of Samaria?" (For Jews have no dealings with Samaritans.) Jesus answered her, "If you knew the gift of God, and who it is that is saying to you, 'Give me a drink,' you would have asked him, and he would have given you living water." The woman said to him, "Sir, you have nothing to draw water with, and the well is deep. Where do you get that living water? Are you greater than our father Jacob? He gave us the well and drank from it himself, as did his sons and his livestock." Jesus said to her, "Everyone who drinks of this water will be thirsty again, but whoever drinks of the water that I will give him will never be thirsty again. The water that I will give him will become in him a spring of water welling up to eternal life." The woman said to him, "Sir, give me this

EXPERIENCING JESUS THROUGH THE EYES OF THE SAMARITAN WOMAN

water, so that I will not be thirsty or have to come here to draw water. (John 4:5–15)

As Jesus listened to this woman, it showed her He truly cared for her as a person. Jesus made her feel she was the most important person in the world. He gave her His 100 percent attention. As Jesus listened to her, He was able to respond with thought provoking questions. Have you ever been talking to someone, and you can just tell they are only talking to you to kill time or while waiting on someone else? As your talking to someone, they are looking around or seem to have something else on their mind. How does it make you feel? Think about how this woman felt when Jesus gave her His undivided attention and made her feel like she was the most important person in the world. Remember, this woman was isolated from the rest of the women in her village, which means none of them would give her the time of the day, and now this Jewish man is intently having a conversation with her and is listening to her as though He really cares for her and really cares what she has to say. This must have truly made her feel very special.

As we seek to live on mission and build relationships with people, we must actively and intently listen to them. We must be good listeners. When we listen to others it shows them we value them as a person and value their thoughts and opinions. When we listen to others we show them we care, which leads to their trust and usually leads to them letting their guards down and letting us into their lives. Harvey Turner stated, "Make the conversation about them. Get to know them, their aspirations, dreams, disappointments, and questions."[48] Intently listening to people opens up opportunities to have conversations with people who may believe differently than we do. It allows us to hear what they are saying and then respond with questions and give our thoughts.

Christians can come across as hateful, judging, and having no care for other people's thoughts and beliefs. If we sit down with peo-

---

[48] Harvey Turner, *Friend of Sinners: An Approach to Evangelism* (Houston, TX: Lucid Books, 2016), 65–66.

ple and listen to their stories, their beliefs, and their thoughts, it not only shows them we value their thoughts, even if we disagree, but it allows us the opportunity to ask questions and give our thoughts as well. For example, if I sit down with a Muslim and truly seem to want to hear more about their religion and their beliefs, this shows them respect and also that I really do want to learn more about them and their religion, but it also gives me the opportunity to ask questions and share my thoughts and beliefs as well. Listening to people usually gives us the rite of passage to speak into their lives more than if they feel we do not really care about them and just want to give them our opinions.

Another positive to actively and intently listening to people is it gives us opportunities to hear their story or their beliefs or their problems and then be able to respond in a way that can bring the truth of the gospel into the conversation. As Jesus listened to this woman, He was able to steer the gospel from a normal conversation to a gospel conversation. By Jesus listening to her and showing her He really cared for her, He was able to move the conversation from "physical water" to a deeper conversation about "living water." By Jesus listening to her, Jesus was able to speak truth in her life that He would not have earned if He had not first listened and cared for her. Jesus was able to speak the truth about her sin, and He was also able to speak the truth about the answer to her sin, which was Himself.

If we want the opportunity to speak the truth into someone else's life, both their sin and the gospel, then we must first be like Jesus and listen to them and care for them. One day I was having lunch with my friend, and I was sharing how much God had blessed me and my family, and then he told me how he wished God would bless his life, but his life was too messed up. He told me how he had cheated on his wife among other things he had done in his life. After I listened to him, I was able to share with him how the gospel of Jesus Christ is good news for him as much as it is for me. I told him how God can save him, forgive him, and how he can have a relationship with God, who can also restore his family and his life if he desires.

I believe the only reason I was able to share this truth was because, by listening to him, I was able to show him how I really cared about him and what he was going through. By listening to him, I was able to hear his problems and then respond with the truth that the answer to all his problems was the good news of the gospel. I was able to speak the truth about his sin and also the truth to the answer to his problem, which is the gospel. Listening to him was the key. If people feel we truly do not care about them and are not really interested in them and what they have to say, we will never earn the right to speak into their lives, which means we will never be able to share the gospel with them.

In the book *Conversational Evangelism*, David and Normal Geisler stated,

> Sometimes we miss opportunities to help nonbelievers take a step closer to Christ because we aren't listening to them carefully enough and miss key ideas that could springboard to deeper spiritual dialogue. You may even be surprised at how easy it is to take normal everyday conversations and turn them into opportunities to share the gospel with others.[49]

In the book *Invitation to Evangelism*, Timothy Beougher stated, "If we really listen to people, we will get to know them better and usually they will say something that gives me an avenues or an open door to bring spiritual things into the conversation."[50]

Conclusion

When it comes to living on mission and engaging people with gospel conversations, we must learn to be good listeners. Listening is a discipline, and we have to discipline ourselves to be better listeners, especially when it comes to evangelism. Jesus listened intently to the

---

[49] David Geisler and Normal Geisler, *Conversational Evangelism: Connecting with People to Share Jesus* (Eugene, OR: Harvest House Publishing, 2014), 36.

[50] Timothy Beougher, *Invitation to Evangelism: Sharing the Gospel with Compassion and Conviction* (Grand Rapids, MI: Kregel Academic, 2021), 184.

Samaritan woman. He showed her He cared for her, and He truly wanted to get to know her. I believe because Jesus did this, she let her guard down and allowed Him into her life. As we engage people with general conversation, we need to intently listen to them. We need to show them that we really care about them, that we really want to get to know them and hear their story. If we do this, they let their guard down and allow us into their lives.

As we engage with people and listen to them and their stories, we have opportunities to respond and ask questions. As Jesus listened to this woman, He was able to respond and ask questions. As Jesus continued to ask questions, He got to know her more and heard her story, and then He was able to start to ask deeper questions, which would eventually lead Him to lead her to a gospel conversation. As we listen to people and ask questions, we get to know them more, and as we hear their stories, we can ask deeper questions that hopefully lead to opportunities to bring the truth of the gospel into the conversation.

As we engage people and hear their stories, we can identify with them and then have the opportunity to share with them how we deal with our problems or where we find hope. For example, let's say I am talking to someone who just found out they were going to have a child born with Down syndrome. As a Christian, I would have the opportunity to tell them how I initially felt overwhelmed and scared, but I put all my trust in God to take care of my son. I would also have the opportunity to tell them how my wife and I live day by day, not knowing what tomorrow will bring for our family and my child, but our trust and our hope are in God. As Christians, we can identify with people. It may not be the exact thing they are going through, but you can still share some of the things you have been through and how you have gotten through them and where your hope is. This gives you the opportunity to bring the gospel into these conversations.

I heard a pastor say when it comes to having gospel conversations, we need to listen to people's stories and then share with them what their story would look like through the eyes of the gospel. Basically, we need to retell their story redemptively. Joshua Chatraw in the book *Telling a Better Story* reveals how the gospel is the answer to what the world is looking for.[51] The gospel story gives the world a greater purpose than just living and dying. The gospel story gives us a better self. Chatraw stated, "The good news of Christianity is that we can know and live in a right relationship with the one who will always prove stable and rather than destroying us, will sustain, love and care for us."[52] The gospel story also gives us a better happiness. Jesus taught the way to find true joy is to deny ourselves and love God above everything and to love others. The way to find complete joy is to deny ourselves to pursue a relationship with Jesus Christ.[53] The truth is that the world is looking for purpose, hope, and joy; but the world is looking for all these things in the wrong place. As Christians, we have what they are looking for, and His name is Jesus. With Jesus in your life, the gospel story becomes your story, and there is no better story in your life than the one only the gospel can give you.

---

[51] Joshua D. Chatraw, *Telling a Better Story: How to Talk About God in a Skeptical Age* (Grand Rapids, MI: Zondervan Academics, 2020).
[52] Ibid., 90.
[53] Ibid., 110.

4

Jesus Showed Love and Compassion

> The Lord is merciful and gracious, slow to anger and abounding in steadfast love. He will not always chide, nor will he keep his anger forever. He does not deal with us according to our sins, nor repay us according to our sins, nor repay us according to our iniquities. For as high as the heavens are above the earth, so great is his steadfast love toward those who fear him; as far as the east is from the west, so far does he remove our transgressions form us. As a father shows compassion to his children, so the Lord show compassion to those who fear him. (Psalm 103:8–13)

One day, I received a call from my friend, and he asked me to meet him for lunch. I agreed, and the next day, we met for lunch. During lunch, he shared with me how him and his wife were getting a divorce. He admitted to me that he had not been the best husband to her. He admitted to me how he had cheated on her at least once, if not more. As we continued with our lunch, I told him how much I hated to hear what his family was going through. I did not agree with what he had done, but instead of condemning him or raining down judgment on him, I just showed him support and love and compassion. I shared the gospel with him and told him how much

EXPERIENCING JESUS THROUGH THE EYES OF THE SAMARITAN WOMAN

Jesus loves him and how Jesus loves him so much He died for him. I also told him how he can be forgiven through the gospel and how I believed there was still hope for his family and marriage through the gospel. He did not accept Christ that day, but at least I do believe he felt he had a friend, someone who really cared for him, someone who would be there for them. Did I want him to believe the gospel? Yes, but I wanted him to understand and believe that my friendship was not based on him believing in the gospel. I remember telling him that I wanted him to know the gospel is true and for him, but him believing what I believe did not dictate my friendship. I told him that I was praying for him, that I cared for him, and that I would always be there for him no matter what.

I believe when it comes to missional living, we need to show love and care for people that is not determinate on them becoming a Christian. Should we want them to become a believer? Yes. Should we share the gospel with them? Yes. Should this dictate our friendship, love, and care for them? I do not think so. I believe if we only are showing love and care for people to share the gospel with them and nothing more people will see right through this. If people feel they are just a project they will see this, and this will probably destroy any opportunity for a friendship and I believe it will destroy any opportunity to share and show them the gospel. Lesslie Newbigin stated, "No one is going to listen to your evangelism unless he sees that it comes out of a fellowship that cares."[54] Bruce Milne stated, "Our failures in evangelism are so often failures in love. Nothing is so guaranteed to draw others to share our 'living water' than an awareness that we genuinely care about them. People want to know that we care before they care about what we know."[55]

As Jesus engaged the Samaritan woman, He showed her love and compassion. How did Jesus show her love and compassion? First, when He approached her, she was startled. In verse 9, the woman stated, "'How is it that you a Jew, ask for a drink from me, a woman

---

[54] Lesslie Newbigin, *A Word in Season* (Grand Rapids, MI: Eerdmans Publishing, 1994).

[55] Bruce Milne, *The Bible Speaks Today: The Message of John,* John Stott, ed. (Downers Grove, IL: IVP Academic, 1981), 86.

of Samaria?'" Jesus, a Jew approached a Samaritan woman. This did not happen in this culture. We discussed this earlier in the book, but the Jews and the Samaritans did not like each other. A Jew would have never approached and engaged a Samaritan, and in this culture, a man would have never approached a woman. So when Jesus engaged with this woman, He was crossing ethical and gender boundaries. Tony Evans stated,

> Even though none of the other Jews would go through Samaria. He went through Samaria, Even though none of the other Jews would drink from the Samaritans woman's cup, He drank from her cup. The Samaritan woman clearly recognized Jesus as a Jew, but He also entered her world. He did so because He was there representing something much bigger.[56]

Andrew MacLaren stated,

> When these words were spoken, the then-known civilized world was cleft by great, deep gulfs of separation, like the crevasses in a glacier, by the side of which our racial animosities and class differences are merely superficial cracks on the surface. Language, religion, national animosities, differences of condition, and saddest of all, difference of sex, split the world up into alien fragments. A 'stranger' and an 'enemy' were expressed in one language, by the same word. The learned and the unlearned, the slave and his master, the barbarian and the Greek, the man

---

[56] Tony Evans, *Oneness Embraced: Reconciliation, the Kingdom, and We Are Stronger Together* (Chicago, IL: Moody Publishers, 2011), 62.

EXPERIENCING JESUS THROUGH THE EYES OF THE SAMARITAN WOMAN

and the woman, stood on opposite sides of the gulfs, flinging hostility across.[57]

Where many in this culture would have never crossed these barriers, Jesus did. Jesus showed this woman love and compassion by breaking through these barriers.

Second, as Jesus was engaging this woman, He was very truthful with her. We see this in verses 16–18, "Jesus said to her, 'Go, call your husband, and come here.' The woman answered him, 'I have no husband.' Jesus said to her, 'you are right in saying, 'I have no husband,' for you have had five husbands, and the one you now have is not your husband. What you have said is true.'" Chris Anderson reveals the situation:

> Ouch. Imagine hearing a description of your darkest secrets, with pinpoint accuracy, from the lips of a stranger. I'm sure her heart immediately filled with shame and fear. I wonder if there was also a bit of hope. Jesus' omniscience certainly made an impression on her; she couldn't stop telling others about it once her talk with Jesus ended. (John 4:29, 39)[58]

As Jesus engaged with this woman, He showed her love and compassion by pointing out her sin. Jesus also showed her love and compassion by not condemning her. Jesus was very truthful about her sinful life, but at the same time, He did not judge her or condemn her. He showed her truth through love. Anderson stated,

> He loved her so much that he didn't ignore it; He exposed it to her-and loved her regardless! He allowed her to see her sin to be inexcus-

---

[57] Quoted by Andrew Maclaren, Kent Hughes, *Preaching the Word: John* (Wheaton, IL: Crossway, 1999), 105.
[58] Chris Anderson, *The God Who Satisfies: How Jesus Seeks, Saves and Satisfies Samaritan Woman—Like Us* (Church Works, 2016), 63–64.

ably vile. He didn't bring the balm of His grace until He brought the lance of the Law. She was immoral. Guilty. Condemned. Without excuse. And she needed to own it before she could be saved from it.[59]

Barrs stated, "Jesus approached the Samaritan woman graciously. He speaks to her with grace and gentleness even about her sin, which clearly weighs heavily upon her."[60]

We see Jesus do the very same thing with the woman caught in adultery in John 8.

> The scribes and the Pharisees brought a woman who had been caught in adultery, and placing her in the midst they said to him, "Teacher, this woman has been caught in the act of adultery. Now in the law, Moses commanded us to stone such women. So what do you say?" This they said to test him, that they might have some charge to bring against him. Jesus bent down and wrote with his finger on the ground. And as they continued to ask him, he stood up and said to them, "Let him who is without sin among you be the first to throw a stone at her." And once more he bent down and wrote on the ground. But when they heard it, they went away one by one, and Jesus was left alone with the woman standing before him. Jesus stood up and said to her, "Woman, where are they? Has no one condemned you'? She said, No one Lord." And Jesus said, "Neither do I condemn you; go, and from now on sin no more." (John 8:3–11)

---

[59] Ibid.
[60] Jerram Barrs, *Learning Evangelism from Jesus* (Wheaton, IL: Crossway, 2009), 44.

EXPERIENCING JESUS THROUGH THE EYES OF THE SAMARITAN WOMAN

Notice, just like the Samaritan woman, Jesus did not excuse her sin. He was truthful with her, but He did it through love and compassion. He did not condemn them or judge them, but He spoke truth in their lives through love and compassion. Think about how these women must have both felt as Jesus showed them love and compassion as their culture showed them hate. Imagine how they felt when Jesus did not condemn, when their culture judged and condemned. Jesus was truthful yet loving because Jesus is love, and He loves all people including these two women. If you are reading this book and maybe are exploring Christianity, I hope you can see through these two women that Jesus loves you, and He wants to remove your guilt or shame. He wants to forgive you and save you; and He wants to give you peace, hope, joy, and life now and for eternity. Jesus also loves you so much that He wants you to know the truth of the gospel of how He came and died on the cross for your sins so that you can be forgiven of your sins, saved from your sins, reconciled back to a relationship with God, and have life. I hope you see and feel Jesus' love for you right now.

As Christians seek to live missionally and engage the world with the gospel of Jesus Christ, we must be truthful, which we will cover in chapter 5, but we must also be loving and compassionate. I personally believe this is one truth that the church, overall, may often get wrong. I personally believe this is one of the reasons the world has turned its back on the church and has called us hypocrites because we have been very truthful, judgmental and condemning, and condemning but have not been loving.

At the Desiring God 2009 Conference for Pastors, Matt Chandler shared an illustration in his sermon.

> He stated he was a freshman in college and he was sitting next to a 26 year single mother trying to get her degree. We began a dialogue about the grace and mercy of Christ in the cross. Some other guys and I would go over and babysit her child and try to talk to her. A friend of mine was in a band playing in the area and we invited her

> to hear him. She agreed. The minister got up and said we would talk about sex. He took a rose, smelled it and threw it out in the crowd and told them to smell the rose. He then began one of the worst, most horrific handlings of what sex is and isn't that I ever sat through. As he wrapped up, he asked, "Where is my rose?" Some kid brought the rose back and it was broken. His point was to hold up the rose and say, "Who wants this rose?" Anger welled up within me and I wanted to say, "Jesus wants the rose!" While we were yet sinners, Christ died for us.[61]

Now imagine if you were this woman that Chandler referred to sitting in that congregation and you heard that. How bad and shameful might you feel? Do you feel this woman would ever walk back into a church again? Probably not. How do you feel this woman might have felt or thought about the church? Or Jesus?

In the book *Dream with Me* by John Perkins, he shares a story of a guy who did a research project where they went out to the community and asked them what they think of when they heard different words. They said words like snow, eagles, teenagers etc. Then they said *Christian*. "He said people stopped in their tracks. They stated words like fake, hypocrites, boring. No one said love or grace or community." He goes on to say he continues to see people rejecting God because of the mess they see in the church. Perkins then goes on to say, "People see the church as a place that condemns rather than loves. They hear voices of hate rather than of redemption and reconciliation."[62]

As we seek to engage the world, like Jesus, we must be truthful, yet we must be loving because Jesus loves all people and all people are made in the image of God. Remember the song you may have

---

[61] Sermon by Matt Chandler at Desiring God 2009 Conference for Pastors.
[62] John Perkins, *Dream with Me: Race, Love, and the Struggle We Must Win* (Grand Rapids, MI: Baker Books, 2017), 189.

grown up to: "Jesus loves the little children of the world. Red, yellow, black, and white—they are precious in His sight. Jesus loves the little children of the world." As we seek to live on mission and engage the world, we must show them love and compassion. We must serve them, care for them, pray for them, and love them the way Jesus did during His ministry and the way He loves them even now. I especially believe this is true in the culture today who are very resistant to the gospel, to religion, and to the church.

This is especially true for the LBGTQ community who, most of the time, are only condemned and judged by Christians and never loved by them. Let me be clear, loving on them and caring for them is not approving of their lifestyle, but I believe in order to reach them with the gospel of Jesus Christ, we must show them a different Christian than they are looking for. They are looking for Christians who only want to hate them, judge them, condemn them, and tell them joyfully they are going to hell. In order to reach them, we must show them a different Christian who loves them, cares for them, serves them, and again shares with them the truth of the gospel, which is another way we show our love for the world, even though the world may not agree.

I remember a few years ago, my neighbors were selling their house and it sold pretty quickly, but then all of a sudden, it went back on the market but quickly sold again. I was talking to my neighbor and they and they made a statement to me, saying how I was lucky the first couple's offer fell through and they did not get the house. He went on to tell me they were a lesbian couple. After I heard this, I first felt relieved thinking now I do not have to live by them and see their lifestyle. I was not going to explain to my son why there is no husband or daddy in the home. At first I felt relieved and then it hit me that even though there would have been challenges, such as what I already have discussed, but I may have had the opportunity to show them a different Christian than what they might think or may have experienced. I may have had the opportunity to love on them, care for them, and I may have just had a chance to be truthful with them that hopefully may have led them to witnessing, hearing, and believing the gospel of Jesus Christ.

Conclusion

As we seek to live on mission and engage the world with the gospel of Jesus Christ, we must be not only like Jesus and be truthful but also loving and compassionate. As we engage the world, we must love them, care for them, and serve them because Jesus loves and cares for them and He has sent us to be his representative in this world and so we must honor Him and represents Him well by how we engage the world. What if we engage the world with hate, judgment, and condemnation? First, we will not be honorably representing Jesus. Second, we will not draw them to Jesus but push them away from Him. Third, we will not have the opportunity to be a witness to Jesus and be able to share the gospel with them. That is exactly what we see with Jesus with these two women. He was loving and not hateful; He showed them grace and not condemnation, and because of this, He drew them close to Himself and opened their hearts and minds to the gospel. I believe because of Jesus showing the Samaritan woman love and compassion, her heart was softened, and she, at that moment, saw who Jesus was and she believed. Why do I say this? After Jesus pointed out her sin, she goes on to say in verse 19 that she perceived Jesus was a prophet. Then in verse 25, I believe she is beginning to recognize Jesus as the Messiah because He says when the Messiah comes He will know all things, and at that moment in verse 26, Jesus tells her that He is the Messiah. In verse 28, the woman left her water jar and ran into her village and told the people to come and see this man Jesus who told her all about herself. Verse 39 reveals the people believed because of the woman's testimony. I again believe the reason this woman's heart was open to the gospel was because Jesus shared the truth, but He shared the truth in love and compassion, and because of this, she believed.

To be honest, the world is looking for Christians who are hateful, judgmental, condemning, and hypocritical. They hate this Christian, they want nothing to do with this Christian, and when they hate and want nothing to do with this Christian, then they hate and want nothing to do with the Jesus this Christian represents. Barrs stated,

> How can we respect people or be gentle, some Christians will protest, when their lives are characterized by sin? Their sin is offensive to heaven, and offensive to us. In responding to this protest, we need to reflect once more on how sweetly and gentle Jesus draws the Samaritan woman to himself-although he is fully aware of the moral disaster of her life.[63]

We all need to remember that we were all once lost and our lives were a wreck, sinful, and offensive to God; but God, in his mercy and grace, saved us, forgave us, and reconciled us back to Himself. Jesus showed us love and compassion when He could have showed us condemnation. Jesus came to us with grace and gentleness just like this woman. Jesus died on the cross for us just like this woman. Barrs reminds us,

> Jesus shows us our sin without making us feel rejected and condemned in his holy presence. Instead, he causes us to know that we are loved, forgiven, welcomed, and accepted, just as he accepts this lonely woman. He welcomes us to sit at his table and to eat with him and he intends to serve us at the Marriage Supper of the Lamb. In the meantime, he desires that we love our neighbors as ourselves, whoever our neighbor may be, and that we relate to them with gentleness and grace.[64]

---

[63] Jerram Barrs, *Learning Evangelism From Jesus* (Wheaton, IL: Crossway, 2009), 48.
[64] Ibid., 50.

Jesus was different, so let's be different. Let's be a different Christian than the world is looking for. Let's be truthful and let's be loving and compassionate; and if we do this, I believe we will draw them to the real Jesus and the real gospel that they truly need. Jesus truly does love and want the rose. The rose desperately needs Jesus.

5

Jesus Fellowshipped

Then I heard what seemed to be the voice of a great multitude, like the roar of many waters and like the sound of mighty peals of thunder, crying out, "Hallelujah! For the Lord our God the Almighty reigns. Let us rejoice and exult and give him the glory, for the marriage of the Lamb has come, and his Bride has made herself ready; it was granted her to clothe herself with fine linen, bright and pure"—for the fine linen is the righteous deeds of the saints. And the angel said to me, "Write this: Blessed are those who are invited to the marriage supper of the Lamb." And he said to me, "These are the true words of God." Then I fell down at his feet to worship him, but he said to me, "You must not do that! I am a fellow servant with you and your brothers who hold to the testimony of Jesus. Worship God." For the testimony of Jesus is the spirit of prophecy. (Revelation 19:6–10)

In the book *The Gospel Comes with a House Key*, Rosaria Butterfield was a radical leftist lesbian who researched and attacked Christians for "hating gays."[65] She ended up meeting a pastor named Ken and his wife, who invited her to dinner and over meals they would show her compassion. They would listen to her and talk openly about sexuality and politics. They were not judging her or made her feel like a project, but a normal human being who they wanted to be friends with. She was overwhelmed with how much they cared and loved her. She would have never expected to be treated this way by Christians. For two years, she continued to go over to their house and visit with them. Through her relationship with this family, she began to see and understand the love of Christ. This would eventually leader her to coming to faith in Christ. She left her gay lifestyle and is now married. Listen to what she says about this pastor and his wife. "They entered my world. They met my friends. We did book exchanges. We talked openly about sexuality and politics. They did not act as if such conversations were polluting them. They did not treat me like a blank slate."[66]

One of the main goals with living on mission is to attempt to get to know lost people and build a relationship with them with the hopes it will lead to a gospel conversation. One way to do this is to leverage your home. A couple of years ago, my family sold our home, and God blessed us with an amazing home that really was more room than we needed. As we moved in, we prayed that God would use our home for opportunities for ministries. Since we have moved in, we have hosted missionaries for meals, led Bible studies for college students, and young professionals; and we have had couples over and had gospel conversations. We have only been in this home for a short period of time, and God has already answered our prayer abundantly.

---

[65] Rosaria Butterfield, *The Gospel Comes with a House Key: Practicing Radically Ordinary Hospitality in Our Post-Christian World* (Wheaton, IL: Crossway, 2018).

[66] Rosaria Butterfield, "My Train Wreck Conversion," *Christianity Today*, February 7, 2013, http://www.christianitytoday.com/ct/2013/january-february/my-train-wreck-conversion.html.

EXPERIENCING JESUS THROUGH THE EYES OF THE SAMARITAN WOMAN

Having people over to your home may be one of the best ways to live on mission. Rosaria Butterfield stated,

> Home is the most important evangelistic instrument in the believers tool kit, especially if our goal is to reach people far from God. The home is where unbelievers can feel warmth of God's acceptance. The home is where they can see our way of life up close enough to ask a reason for the hope that enlivens us. The home is where we turn "strangers into neighbors and neighbors into family."[67]

As you leverage your home for missional living, share a meal with people. Sharing a meal with someone is one of the most effective and easiest ways to get to know them, and they to get to know you. Sharing a meal oftentimes will let their guard down, and they may be more open to letting you into their lives. Dustin Willis and Brandon Clements stated,

> In our increasingly hostile culture, the importance of hospitality cannot be overstated. And we are not suggesting that you go silent on all your beliefs and values. We've found that those conversations tend to be more effective when they happen in a clear context of grace and love over meals than in a shouting matches from afar.[68]

One of the most effective way we see Jesus living on mission was through sharing a meal with them.

---

[67] Rosaria Butterfield, *The Gospel Comes with a House Key: Practicing Radically Ordinary Hospitality in Our Post-Christian World* (Wheaton, IL: Crossway, 2018), 63.

[68] Dustin Willis and Brandon Clements, *The Simplest Way to Change the World: Biblical Hospitality As a Way of Life* (Chicago, IL: Moody Publishers, 2017), 64.

In verses 7–11, we see Jesus fellowshipping with the woman:

> A woman from Samaria came to draw water. Jesus said to her, "Give me a drink." (For his disciples had gone away into the city to buy food.) The Samaritan woman said to him, "How is it that you, a Jew, ask for a drink from me, a woman of Samaria?" (For Jews have no dealings with Samaritans.) Jesus answered her, "If you knew the gift of God, and who it is that is saying to you, 'Give me a drink,' you would have asked him, and he would have given you living water." The woman said to him, "Sir, you have nothing to draw water with, and the well is deep. Where do you get that living water"? As Jesus asked her for a drink of water, He was fellowshipping with her. Notice she was startled as Jesus asked her. She said "how is that you a Jew would ask me for a drink." A Jew would never ask a Samaritan for a drink of water and a Jew would especially never ask to share the same cup as a Samaritan. This would have never happened, but what Jesus did was show us a very intimate act of fellowship. The word translated "dealings" means to use the same utensils.

John MacArthur stated, "Jesus was willing to ceremonially defile Himself by drinking from her water pot."[69]

Tony Evans stated, "Jewish lips on her Samaritan cup was an intimate act of fellowship and warm acceptance. It was something that wasn't done in this woman's neighborhood. Not only was this an

---

[69] John MacArthur, *The MacArthur New Testament Commentary: John 1–11* (Chicago, IL: Moody Publishers, 2006), 144.

action that signified a willingness for fellowship, but it was also an action that gave the woman value."[70]

Put yourself in this woman's shoes. How would you have felt? Think about this. You are a woman that comes to get water in the hottest part of the day to avoid people. You are isolated from the rest of the women in your village, and as you are getting water, a Jewish man approaches you and not only talks to you, but he wants to share a cup of water with you. I think there is a reason why Jesus was able to have a longer conversation that eventually led to a spiritual conversation. He is probably the first person in a long time to seem to care about her. When it comes to living on mission, we must meet people, spend time with them, and fellowship with them. When we do this, God can and will use this to soften and open their hearts so they will allow you into their lives and be open to a deeper conversation. I think this is what we see going on in this story.

Because Jesus spent time with her, He was able to speak truth to her. He was able to move into a deeper conversation with her through his fellowship with her. Tony Evans stated,

> Jesus was able to turn a general conversation into an evangelistic opportunity because he was willing to spend time with her. He was willing to drink from her cup. Because of this he was able to witness to her soul. If he had not been willing to do these things, he would not have had the ability to talk to her spiritually.[71]

We see Jesus do this all throughout His ministry. He was always living on mission by fellowshipping with people, and His number one way was to share a meal with them. Butterfield stated, "The vast majority of Jesus' personal encounters with lost people happened over meals in homes. In the gospels, Jesus seems to be always coming

---

[70] Tony Evans, *Oneness Embraced: Reconciliation, the Kingdom, and We Are Stronger Together* (Chicago, IL: Moody Publishers, 2011), 61.

[71] Tony Evans, *Oneness Embraced: Reconciliation, the Kingdom, and We Are Stronger Together* (Chicago, IL: Moody Publishers, 2011), 64.

from a meal, at one or on his way to one. He pretty much eats his way through the Gospel of Luke."[72]

"The Son of Man has come eating and drinking, and you say, 'Look at him! A glutton and a drunkard, a friend of tax collectors and sinners!'" (Luke 7:34). Jesus was so much into eating and drinking that the Jewish leaders accused Him of doing this too much. Tim Chester, in his book *A Meal With Jesus*, stated,

> Jesus is called a glutton and a drunkard, a friend of tax collectors and sinners. This is why eating and drinking were so important in the mission of Jesus: they were a sign of his friendship with tax collectors and sinners. His "excess" of food and "excess" of grace are linked. In the ministry of Jesus, meals were enacted grace, community and mission.[73]

Sharing a meal can be an easy and great way to live on mission because it gives you the opportunity to share the gospel through your words and show the gospel through your life. Chester stated, "I don't want to reduce church and mission to meals, but I do want to argue that meals should be an integral and significant part of our shared life. They represent it: they embody and enact our mission. Community and mission are more than meals, but it's hard to conceive of them without meals."[74]

> After this he went out and saw a tax collector named Levi, sitting at the tax booth. And he said to him, "Follow me." And leaving everything, he rose and followed him. And Levi made him

---

[72] Rosaria Butterfield, *The Gospel Comes with a House Key: Practicing Radically Ordinary Hospitality in Our Post-Christian World* (Wheaton, IL: Crossway, 2018), 63.

[73] Tim Chester, *A Meal with Jesus: Discovering Grace, Community, and Mission Around the Table* (Wheaton, IL: Crossway, 2011), 14.

[74] Ibid.

EXPERIENCING JESUS THROUGH THE EYES OF THE SAMARITAN WOMAN

> a great feast in his house, and there was a large company of tax collectors and others reclining at table with them. And the Pharisees and their scribes grumbled at his disciples, saying, "Why do you eat and drink with tax collectors and sinners?" And Jesus answered them, "Those who are well have no need of a physician, but those who are sick. I have not come to call the righteous but sinners to repentance." (Luke 5:27–32)

In this text, we see Jesus call Levi to follow Him and then we see Jesus and Levi sharing a meal with tax collectors and sinners. Tax collectors were social outcasts who were hated by the Jews because they worked for the Romans and cheated the Jews out of money. Chester reminds us that because these tax collectors sided with the Romans they ultimately were enemies of God so basically God was fellowshipping with His enemies.[75] Chester stated, "When Jesus eats with Levi, the message is clear: Jesus has come for losers, people on the margins, people who've made a mess of their lives, people who are ordinary."[76]

> One of the Pharisees asked him to eat with him, and he went into the Pharisee's house and reclined at table. And behold, a woman of the city, who was a sinner, when she learned that he was reclining at table in the Pharisee's house, brought an alabaster flask of ointment, and standing behind him at his feet, weeping, she began to wet his feet with her tears and wiped them with the hair of her head and kissed his feet and anointed them with the ointment. Now when the Pharisee who had invited him saw this, he said to him-

---

[75] Tim Chester, *A Meal with Jesus: Discovering Grace, Community and Mission Around the Table* (Wheaton, IL: Crossway, 2011), 19.
[76] Ibid., 31.

self, "If this man were a prophet, he would have known who and what sort of woman this is who is touching him, for she is a sinner." And Jesus answering said to him, "Simon, I have something to say to you." And he answered, "Say it, Teacher." "A certain moneylender had two debtors. One owed five hundred denarii, and the other fifty. When thy could not pay, he cancelled the debt of both. Now which of them will love him more?" Simon answered, "The one, I suppose, for whom he cancelled the larger debt." And he said to him, "You have judged rightly." Then turning toward the woman he said to Simon, "Do you see this woman? I entered your house; you gave me no water for my feet, but she has wet my feet with her tears and wiped them with her hair. You gave me no kiss, but from the time I came in she has not ceased to kiss my feet. You did not anoint my head with oil, but she has anointed my feet with ointment. Therefore I tell you, her sins, which are many, are forgiven—for she loved much. But he who is forgiven little, loves little." And he said to her, "Your sins are forgiven." Then those who were at table with him began to say among themselves, "Who is this, who even forgives sins?" And he said to the woman, "Your faith has saved you; go in peace." (Luke 7:36–50)

Jesus goes to the home of a Pharisee, and while He is there, a woman comes in and begins to wipe Jesus' feet with her tears, her hair and then anoints His feet with an alabaster flask of ointment. This woman was a sinner, so to the Pharisee, this woman was like a disease that he would do whatever he could to stay away from her, but Jesus would show her love and compassion. This woman was demonstrating an act of intimacy toward Jesus and the Pharisee is appalled at how Jesus is letting this woman do this. Jesus then uses

EXPERIENCING JESUS THROUGH THE EYES OF THE SAMARITAN WOMAN

this moment to speak the truth to Simon. Jesus contrasts this woman's acts compared to Simon's inactivity.

Simon offered no water to Jesus, and this woman wet Jesus' feet. Simon offered no kiss to Jesus, and this woman continuously kissed Jesus' feet. Simon did not anoint Jesus' head, and this woman anointed His feet. During this time, a good host would have offered their guest water and a kiss, but this man, Simon, did not do these. This woman was a better host than Simon even in Simon's own home. Jesus then goes on to use a parable to teach Simon about the relationship between love and forgiveness. If someone forgives you, you will love them, and if someone forgives you a lot, then you will love them a lot. Chester stated,

> The difference between Simon and the woman is not just how they view Jesus. It's also how they view themselves. Simon has no sense of forgiveness, because he has no sense of need. But the woman has a strong sense of her brokenness. She knows her life is a mess. And she sees Jesus as someone who accepts her anyway. She has an overwhelming love for him-a love that risks social disgrace.[77]

In this story, Jesus uses a meal to reveal the truth that if we truly have experienced God's love, grace, and forgiveness, then we will truly extend love, grace, and forgiveness to others. This woman truly experienced love and grace that Jesus showed her, and it was seen through her love for Jesus.

> Now as they went on their way, Jesus entered a village. And a woman named Martha welcomed him into her house. And she had a sister called Mary, who sat at the Lord's feet and lis-

---

[77] Tim Chester, *A Meal with Jesus: Discovering Grace, Community and Mission Around the Table* (Wheaton, IL: Crossway, 2011), 45.

> tened to his teaching. But Martha was distracted with much serving. And she went up to him and said, "Lord, do you not care that my sister has left me to serve alone? Tell her then to help me." But the Lord answered her, "Martha, Martha, you are anxious and troubled about many things, but one thing is necessary. Mary has chosen the good portion, which will not be taken away from her." (Luke 10:38–42)

Jesus goes to Mary and Martha's home for a meal. As Jesus arrives, Martha is busy getting everything ready for the meal. Martha is mad because she is busy with getting everything ready, but instead of helping, Mary is sitting at Jesus' feet, spending time with him. Martha goes to Jesus to get Him to tell Mary to help her, but Jesus uses this opportunity to teach Martha something very important. He teaches Martha how it is okay and important to serve others, but the most important thing in the world is to spend time with Jesus. Thabiti Anyabwile stated, "Jesus says to Martha and everyone: In all your busyness don't forget that only one thing is necessary. That one thing is not the next task on your to-do list. That one thing is not serving others. The one necessary thing is enjoying the Lord Himself."[78]

> While Jesus was speaking, a Pharisee asked him to dine with him, so he went in and reclined at table. The Pharisee was astonished to see that he did not first wash before dinner. And the Lord said to him, "Now you Pharisees cleanse the outside of the cup and of the dish, but inside you are full of greed and wickedness. You fools! Did not he who made the outside make the inside also? But give as alms those things that are within, and behold, everything is clean for

---

[78] Thabiti Anyabwile, *Christ-Centered Exposition: Luke* (Nashville, TN: B&H Publishing, 2018), 185.

you. "But woe to you Pharisees! For you tithe mint and rue and every herb, and neglect justice and the love of God. These you ought to have done, without neglecting the others. Woe to you Pharisees! For you love the best seat in the synagogues and greetings in the marketplaces. Woe to you! For you are like unmarked graves, and people walk over them without knowing it." One of the lawyers answered him, "Teacher, in saying these things you insult us also." And he said, "Woe to you lawyers also! For you load people with burdens hard to bear, and you yourselves do not touch the burdens with one of your fingers. Woe to you! For you build the tombs of the prophets whom your fathers killed. So you are witnesses and you consent to the deeds of your fathers, for they killed them, and you build their tombs. Therefore also the Wisdom of God said, 'I will send them prophets and apostles, some of whom they will kill and persecute,' so that the blood of all the prophets, shed from the foundation of the world, may be charged against this generation, from the blood of Abel to the blood of Zechariah, who perished between the altar and the sanctuary. Yes, I tell you, it will be required of this generation. Woe to you lawyers! For you have taken away the key of knowledge. You did not enter yourselves, and you hindered those who were entering." As he went away from there, the scribes and the Pharisees began to press him hard and to provoke him to speak about many things, lying in wait for him, to catch him in something he might say. (Luke 11:37–53)

In Luke 11:37–53, Jesus shares a meal with another Pharisee and reveals to him how we can be clean on the outside but filthy in the heart. Through a meal, Jesus was revealing the truth that through the gospel our hearts can be cleansed. Anyabwile stated, "The Lord offers this gospel to those who know that their lives are messed up because of sin and that they need a Savior. They know their need for repentance, and they delight to turn to the Lord from sin for his salvation. Those sinners who turn and trust are cleansed by Christ."[79]

> One Sabbath, when he went to dinner at the house of a ruler of the Pharisees, they were watching him carefully. And behold, there was a man before him who had dropsy. And Jesus responded to the lawyers and Pharisees, saying, "Is it lawful to heal on the Sabbath, or not?" But they remained silent. Then he took him and healed him and sent him away. And he said to them, "Which of you, having a son or an ox that has fallen into a well on a Sabbath day, will not immediately pull him out?" And they could not reply to these things. Now he told a parable to those who were invited, when he noticed how they chose the places of honor, saying to them, "When you are invited by someone to a wedding feast, do not sit down in a place of honor, lest someone more distinguished than you be invited by him, and he who invited you both will come and say to you, 'Give your place to this person,' and then you will begin with shame to take the lowest place. But when you are invited, go and sit in the lowest place, so that when your host comes he may say to you, 'Friend, move up higher.' Then you will be honored in the presence of all who sit at table with you. For everyone who exalts himself will be humbled, and he who

---

[79] Thabiti Anyabwile, *Christ-Centered Exposition: Luke* (Nashville, TN: B&H Publishing, 2018), 198.

humbles himself will be exalted." He said also to the man who had invited him, "When you give a dinner or a banquet, do not invite your friends or your brothers or your relatives or rich neighbors, lest they also invite you in return and you be repaid. But when you give a feast, invite the poor, the crippled, the lame, the blind, and you will be blessed, because they cannot repay you. For you will be repaid at the resurrection of the just." When one of those who reclined at table with him heard these things, he said to him, "Blessed is everyone who will eat bread in the kingdom of God!" But he said to him, "A man once gave a great banquet and invited many. And at the time for the banquet he sent his servant to say to those who had been invited, 'Come, for everything is now ready.' But they all alike began to make excuses. The first said to him, 'I have bought a field, and I must go out and see it. Please have me excused.' And another said, 'I have bought five yoke of oxen, and I go to examine them. Please have me excused.' And another said, 'I have married a wife, and therefore I cannot come.' So the servant came and reported these things to his master. Then the master of the house became angry and said to his servant, 'Go out quickly to the streets and lanes of the city, and bring in the poor and crippled and blind and lame.' And the servant said, 'Sir, what you commanded has been done, and still there is room.' And the master said to the servant, 'Go out to the highways and hedges and compel people to come in, that my house may be filled. For I tell you, none of those men who were invited shall taste my banquet.'"
(Luke 14:1–24)

In this story, Jesus is having a meal with a ruler of the Pharisees on the Sabbath, and while He is at this meal, this man comes in who has dropsy. Jesus heals the man and then asked the man if it is lawful to heal on the Sabbath. The man says nothing, and then Jesus takes this opportunity to teach this man a very important truth. Jesus reveals to this man, and to us, two important truths. First, the truth is that we are the poor, the blind, the crippled, and the lame; but through God's grace, He still invites us us to his great banquet. Even though we do not deserve it, or have not earned it and cannot pay Him back, God, in His grace, has sent His Son Jesus to save us from our sin and to be reconciled back to God and has invited us to His banquet. Second, since God has extended His grace upon us, we should offer our grace to others. As we seek to live on mission, we should have a desire to serve and share a meal with those who are in need and who cannot pay us back. We should not see them and serve them as less than us, but we should serve them and see them as equals. This is done by not serving a meal, but sharing a meal.

Christine Pohl stated, "Often we maintain significant boundaries when offering help to persons in need. Many churches prepare and serve meals to hungry neighbors, but few church members find it easy to sit and eat with those who need the meal."[80] Chester stated, "If you tell someone he's a sinner who needs God while you're handing him a cup of soup, then he'll hear you saying he's a loser who should become like you. But when you eat together as friends and you tell him what a messed up person you are, then you can tell him about sin and grace."[81]

> Then came the day of Unleavened Bread, on which the Passover lamb had to be sacrificed. So Jesus sent Peter and John, saying, "Go and prepare the Passover for us, that we may eat it." They said to him, "Where will you have us pre-

---

[80] Christine D. Rohl, *Making Room: Recovering Hospitality as a Christian Tradition* (Grand Rapids, MI: Eerdmans, 1999), 74.
[81] Tim Chester, *A Meal with Jesus: Discovering Grace, Community and Mission Around the Table* (Wheaton, IL: Crossway, 2011), 83.

EXPERIENCING JESUS THROUGH THE EYES OF THE SAMARITAN WOMAN

pare it?" He said to them, "Behold, when you have entered the city, a man carrying a jar of water will meet you. Follow him into the house that he enters and tell the master of the house, 'The Teacher says to you, Where is the guest room, where I may eat the Passover with my disciples?' And he will show you a large upper room furnished; prepare it there." And they went and found it just as he had told them, and they prepared the Passover. And when the hour came, he reclined at table, and the apostles with him. And he said to them, "I have earnestly desired to eat this Passover with you before I suffer. For I tell you I will not eat it until it is fulfilled in the kingdom of God." And he took a cup, and when he had given thanks he said, "Take this, and divide it among yourselves. For I tell you that from now on I will not drink of the fruit of the vine until the kingdom of God comes." And he took bread, and when he had given thanks, he broke it and gave it to them, saying, "This is my body, which is given for you. Do this in remembrance of me." And likewise the cup after they had eaten, saying, "This cup that is poured out for you is the new covenant in my blood. But behold, the hand of him who betrays me is with me on the table. For the Son of Man goes as it has been determined, but woe to that man by whom he is betrayed!" And they began to question one another, which of them it could be who was going to do this. (Luke 22:7–23)

Jesus had gathered with His apostles to celebrate Passover, and as they were sharing the Passover meal, Jesus would teach them and show them the New Covenant that He would make with His people through His death. The bread represents His body which will be broken and the cup represents His blood which will be shed. Jesus then tells them, and us, to do this in remembrance of Him. The Lord's Supper is a reminder of what Jesus has done for us. Jesus died on the cross for us so that we can be saved, forgiven, free, and reconciled back to a relationship with God. Over a meal, Jesus revealed the truth of the gospel with His apostles:

> That very day two of them were going to a village named Emmaus, about seven miles from Jerusalem, and they were talking with each other about all these things that had happened. While they were talking and discussing together, Jesus himself drew near and went with them. But their eyes were kept from recognizing him. And he said to them, "What is this conversation that you are holding with each other as you walk?" And they stood still, looking sad. Then one of them, named Cleopas, answered him, "Are you the only visitor to Jerusalem who does not know the things that have happened there in these days?" And he said to them, "What things?" And they said to him, "Concerning Jesus of Nazareth, a man who was a prophet mighty in deed and word before God and all the people, and how our chief priests and rulers delivered him up to be condemned to death, and crucified him. But we had hoped that he was the one to redeem Israel. Yes, and besides all this, it is now the third day since these things happened. Moreover, some women of our company amazed us. They were at the tomb early in the morning, and when they did not find his body, they came back saying that they had even seen a vision of angels, who said that he was alive. Some of those who were with us went to the tomb and found it just as the women had said, but him they did not see."

EXPERIENCING JESUS THROUGH THE EYES OF THE SAMARITAN WOMAN

> And he said to them, "O foolish ones, and slow of heart to believe all that the prophets have spoken! Was it not necessary that the Christ should suffer these things and enter into his glory?" And beginning with Moses and all the Prophets, he interpreted to them in all the Scriptures the things concerning himself. So they drew near to the village to which they were going. He acted as if he were going farther, but they urged him strongly, saying, "Stay with us, for it is toward evening and the day is now far spent." So he went in to stay with them. When he was at table with them, he took the bread and blessed and broke it and gave it to them. And their eyes were opened, and they recognized him. And he vanished from their sight. They said to each other, "Did not our hearts burn within us while he talked to us on the road, while he opened to us the Scriptures?" And they rose that same hour and returned to Jerusalem. And they found the eleven and those who were with them gathered together, saying, "The Lord has risen indeed, and has appeared to Simon!" Then they told what had happened on the road, and how he was known to them in the breaking of the bread. (Luke 24:13–35)

Jesus appears to these two men on the road to Emmaus, but they did not recognize Him. As Jesus engages them, He asks them a question about this man named Jesus of Nazareth. These men began to tell Him all about how Jesus who they believed was the promised Messiah, but He was crucified by the Jews and the Romans. At this time, it had been three days. These men stated that they heard Jesus' body was missing, but they themselves had not seen. At this time, Jesus began to teach them how the Scriptures had pointed to Jesus. The men ask Jesus to stay with them again, not recognizing Him, but then Jesus broke the bread, and they immediately recognized Him as

Jesus the promised Messiah who had died, but now He is alive. Over a meal, Jesus revealed how even though He died on the cross, He did not stay dead. Jesus rose from the dead, and He is still alive today. Kent Hughes describes the situation:

> How they were jolted! Surprised, Cleopas! Surprise, Mary! Surprise, citizens of Emmaus! Surprise world! Christ is risen! He is risen indeed! That explosive moment was burned into their minds for eternity. And then he was gone. But their hearts were left with Easter fire: "They said to each other, did not our hearts burn within us while we talked to us on the road, while he opened to us the Scriptures?" Their winter of soul was gone forever. So it is when the Scriptures come alive in your soul with the centrality and reality of Jesus.[82]

When it came to missional living, Jesus often used meals as opportunities to get to know people and share the truth with them. Chester stated, "Jesus didn't run projects, establish ministries, create programs, or put on events. He ate meals."[83] Jesus would share meals with the religious prideful, prostitutes, criminals, and the social outcast. Over meals, Jesus would hang out with people, get to know them, and share the truth with them. Jesus used meals to call out people's sins, such as the Pharisees, and Jesus used meals to share the good news of the gospel with people, such as Zacchaeus and the sinful woman. Over many meals, Jesus changed many lives.

As we seek to live on mission like Jesus, we must engage in fellowship. One of the easiest ways for fellowship is to invite people to

---

[82] Kent Hughes, *Preaching the Word: Luke* (Wheaton, IL: Crossway, 2015), 847.

[83] Tim Chester, *A Meal with Jesus: Discovering Grace, Community and Mission Around the Table* (Wheaton, IL: Crossway, 2011), 89.

your home and share a meal with them. When it comes to churches engaging the community, Francis Shaeffer stated,

> Don't start with a big program. Don't suddenly think you can add to your budget and begin. Start personally and start in your home. I dare you. I dare you in the name of Jesus Christ. Do what I am going to suggest. Begin by opening your home for community. You don't need a big program. You don't have to convince your session or board. All you have to do is open your home and begin. And there is no place in God's world where there are no people who will come and share a home as long as it is a real home.[84]

I was talking to a local ministry in Birmingham, and they see the value in utilizing meals to live on mission, so they are starting to meet with people and churches to equip and help their members learn how to have people in your homes, share a meal, and use this time to share and show the gospel of Jesus Christ. Chester also stated, "It's not that meals save people. People are saved through the gospel message. But meals will create natural opportunities powerfully with what you are saying."[85] Andrew Hamilton, in the article "Foods and Friends Night" stated, "Meals bring mission into the ordinary. But that's where most people are—living in the ordinary. That's where we need to go to reach them. We too readily think of mission as extraordinary. Most people live in the ordinary, and most people will be reached by ordinary people."[86]

Like the Samaritan woman, when God's people take time to get to know someone by sharing a meal with them; it makes them

---

[84] Quoted by Drew Goodmanson in a recorded sermon, "Gospel Hospitality: Making Room," Kaleo Church, San Diego, September 2, 2007, www.kaleochurch.com/sermon/gospel-hospitality-making-room.

[85] Ibid.

[86] Andrew Hamilton, "Food and Friends Night," Backyardmissionary.com (blog), June 14, 2006, www.backyardmissionary.com.

feel special. It makes them feel like someone truly cares for them. I believe the reason Jesus was able to have a deeper conversation with the woman was because He first fellowshipped with her and showed her He cared about her and wanted to get to know her. It's the same with us. As we spend time with people and show them how much we care about them and how we truly want to get to know them, they can let their guard and allow us to have a deeper conversation with them that prayerfully will lead to a gospel conversation. Like Jesus, over meals we can have truthful conversations. We can talk about sin and how sin leads us away from God. How sin leads us to a life that God did not create us for. How sin ultimately leads to our destruction and leads us to an eternity away from God. We can also talk about the truth of the good news of the gospel. How the gospel saves us from our sins. How the gospel forgives and heals us from our sins. How the gospel draws us to God. How the gospel leads us to live the life that God created us for. How the gospel brings us complete joy and satisfaction. How the gospel leads us to live a life of flourishing and ultimately gives us life now and for eternity. These are the deep conversation that we can have with people over meals if we just make the time to leverage our home and our tables for the gospel.

In the book *Muslims and Christians at the Table*, Bruce Mcdowell and Anees Zaka explain how in order to engage Muslims with the gospel of Jesus, Christians must spend time with them to show them you care for them and want to truly be their friend.[87] When you do this they will, in return, be your friend, learn to trust you, and listen to you. Hang out with them, play sports with them, and share a meal with them. Mcdowell and Zaka stated,

> They may wonder why you are taking an interest in them. They will be trying to discern your motives. Your 'free gospel smells tainted to people whose trust and respect you have not

---

[87] Bruce A. Mcdowell and Anees Zaka, *Muslims and Christians at the Table: Promoting Biblical Understanding among North American Muslims* (Phillisburg, NJ: P&R Publishing, 1999), 198.

earned.' Your love for people must not be simply intellectual. Remember, Muslims are made in God's image. Your consistent lifestyle of love will earn you the right to be trusted and heard. Love them as Jesus loved you.[88]

As we seek to live on mission through fellowship, what are some ways we can do this well? Host international students in your home. If you live near a college campus, contact them to see if they have an international student welcoming program. Where I live, the local college has lots of international students, and they have a program where you can sign up to host and care for an international student. Invite your neighbors over for dinner. Maybe you currently know your neighbors or not, but this is a great opportunity to get to know them or get to know them better. Invite them over and share a meal with them. Host a Bible study in your home. I do not necessarily mean to invite church friends over, which is not a bad idea, but I mean host a neighborhood Bible study. Put invites into mailboxes, advertise your Bible study on popular neighborhood apps, or put a sign in your yard with the information. Host a "seeking Christianity Bible study." This could be something like the Alpha Bible study that is designed to host at your home and have people come and ask questions about Christianity.

Invite people over for a sporting event. We live in a country that is very "religious" about sports, so I say leverage it for the gospel. Invite your nonbeliever neighbors, friends, and coworkers and use it to share and show the gospel. Some other opportunities to get to know people is to host a game night, host a cookout, host a supper club, host a book club, have people over for movie night, and throw holiday parties. These are all great opportunities to get to know people and to share your life with them. When it comes to fellowshipping with people, the key is to get to know them, show them the real you, and build a friendship and trust that hopefully leads to opportu-

---

[88] Ibid.

nities to have deeper and gospel conversations. The most important thing is to show and share the gospel.

When it comes to living on mission and showing hospitality, Jesus reminds us in Luke 14:12–14:

> He said also to the man, "When you give a dinner or banquet, do not invite your friends or your brothers or your relatives or rich neighbors, lest they also invite you in return and you repaid. But when you give a feast, invite the poor, the crippled, the lame, the blind, and you will be blessed, because they cannot repay you. For you will be repaid at the resurrection of the just."

When you think about leveraging your home for fellowship and living on mission remember those who cannot pay you back. Remember those who are poor, crippled, lame, and the blind.

We must care for orphans and widow. James tells us in 1:27, "Religion that is pure and undefiled before God the Father is this: to visit orphans and widows in their affliction, and to keep oneself unstained from the world." The word *visit* is used other places in Scripture to show how God visits His people, helps them, strengthens them, and encourages them. Basically, what James is saying is more than just to say hello to them, but to really care for them, love them, serve them, and encourage them. James wrote to the Christians to teach them how to live against the culture. The culture caters to the rich and powerful, but the kingdom of God cares for the poor and the needy. James is saying pure religion is caring for those who are poor, who are needy, or who cannot pay you back. The truth is as Christians we should have a desire and passion to care for orphans and widows because it is clear from Scripture that God cares for them, and as His people who share His love, we should care for them as well.

We must care for those abroad who are coming to our backyards. Willis and Clements stated, "There is great need for cross-cultural ministry right here in our own backyards. People from all over the world are visiting and relocating to North America, and odds are, no matter where you live you see an increasing presence who don't look like you. This is a wonderful gospel opportunity."[89] I have to be honest, as I write this my neighbor across the street is from India and even though I have spoken to him across the street, I really have not taken the time to get to know him and his family.

"You shall treat the stranger who sojourns with you as the native among you, and you shall love him as yourself, for you were strangers in the land of Egypt: I am the Lord your God" (Leviticus 19:34). As Christians, we should care for those who do not look like us because God loves them, and as His people, we should love them as well and care for them. Matthew Bennett, in his book *Hope For American Evangelical* stated,

> If a church is to minister to its city as a whole-including all the diverse segments of its composition—its members will need to intentionally transcend those enclaves that are all too easily form around our natural affinities. That will be best accomplished by forging interpersonal relationships that are not limited to convenience and proximity. It will mean inviting people from other neighborhoods to join us for meals in our homes and backyards. It will mean bringing our families to their homes and enjoying fellowship and friendship. A very tangible way to see that happen in a local church, then, is to encourage members to invite people they don't know to come over for a Sunday afternoon lunch rather than choosing to invite their old friends.[90]

---

[89] Dustin Willis and Brandon Clements, *The Simplest Way to Change the World: Biblical Hospitality as a Way of Life* (Chicago, IL: Moody Publishers, 2017), 140.

[90] Matthew Bennett, *Hope For American Evangelicals: A Missionary Perspective on Restoring our Broken House* (Brentwood, TN: B&H Publishing, 2023), 58–59.

Willis and Clements stated,

> You can be a welcoming presence to the ethnic minority or immigrant families you come in contact with. You can volunteer to help international students. You can even get involved with local refugee resettlement programs, which seek to connect refugees with host families to teach them basic things about the culture and be a relational resource to answer questions.[91]

The church we partnered with in Clarkston, Georgia, would come along side refugees and be there to help them get settled into this country. This church would show these refugees the love of Jesus by serving them and being there for them.

We must care for the disabled. When my wife was pregnant with our son, our doctor ran some tests to see if our child was susceptible to any potential birth defects. The results came back that our child could potentially be born with Down syndrome. Our doctor then set us up with a detailed ultrasound where they would look for any markers for Down syndrome. While we were having the ultrasound, we were talking to the doctor about how people with Down syndrome are living more active and longer lives, and during this conversation, the doctor basically told us that, no matter what, our child, if he was born with Down Syndrome, would basically be useless. This is how most of the world thinks about those with disabilities. They often think they are useless, but the good news is that God does not. In John 9:1, Jesus and the disciples come up to a man born blind, and the disciples ask Jesus, "Why is this man born blind? Was it because of his sin or his parents sin?" In this culture, that is what they believed. If a person was born with a disability they or someone in their family had sinned. In verse 3, Jesus says it was not because of sin, but it was so the works of God might be displayed in him. Think

---

[91] Dustin Willis and Brandon Clements, *The Simplest Way to Change the World: Biblical Hospitality as a Way of Life* (Chicago, IL: Moody Publishers, 2017), 140.

about this: this disciples only saw his disability; they only saw his weakness and his problem, but God saw his purpose. I believe God not only loves the disabled, but God has a purpose for them just like He loves us and has a purpose for us. The truth is that when it comes to the disabled, we must care for them and love them because God loves and cares for them. Where the world sees weak and useless, God sees strength and purpose. Ever since Connor has been in our life, there is literally not a day that goes by where I do not see how much God values and loves the disabled.

As we seek to live on mission, let us not forget those who are in need. Let us be intentional in looking for ways to show them hospitality by serving them; invite them over for a meal. Invite them over to your house for a birthday party or any other party. One of the hardest thing my wife and I go is that our son rarely, if ever, gets invited to birthday parties; and he never gets invited over for sleepovers. As Christians, we must do what we can to show them the love of Jesus because Jesus does truly love them and He has a purpose for their lives.

Conclusion

As Jesus asked the Samaritan woman for a drink, He was not only showing her love and compassion, but He was also showing her fellowship. By fellowshipping with the woman, He showed her He cared for her and truly wanted to get to know her. I believe this caused her heart to soften and drew her to Him. She then lowered her guard, trusted Him, let Him into her life; and this led Him to have a deeper conversation with her. If we truly want to live on mission, we must fellowship with people. By fellowshipping with people, it shows them we care about them, and we truly want to get to know them. This causes them to lower their guard, builds their trust in you, and allows you into their lives. This will then allow you to have a deeper conversation with them where you can speak truth in their lives.

One of the best ways to fellowship with people is through sharing a meal. As we share meals with people, it gives us the opportunity to get to know them, build a relationship with them, and have deeper conversations with them. Over meals, we can share the truth with them. We can share the truth about sin, and we can share the truth about the gospel. How the gospel saves us from our sin, forgives us from our sins, cleanses us from our sins, and reconciles us back to a relationship with God; and we can have life—life now and for eternity.

Willis and Clement stated,

> If we walk in this biblical hospitality and view our homes foremost as a gospel weapon, offering our homes for the Holy Spirit to use as He sees fit, there's no telling what could happen. It may not transpire fast and it may not be some glamorous story that goes into a book, but God will do what he promised: He will build His church and draw people to Himself through our ordinary faithfulness to leverage our homes for His mission. It's just that simple.[92]

---

[92] Dustin Willis and Brandon Clements, *The Simplest Way to Change the World: Biblical Hospitality as a Way of Life* (Chicago, IL: Moody Publishers, 2017), 27.

6

Jesus Was truthful

And you were dead in the trespasses and sins in which you once walked, following the course of this world, following the prince of the power of the air, the spirit that is now at work in the sons of disobedience—among whom we all once lived in the passions of our flesh, carrying out the desires of the body and the mind, and were by nature children of wrath, like the rest of mankind. But God, being rich in mercy, because of the great love with which he loved us, even when we were dead in our trespasses, made us alive together with Christ—by grace you have been saved—and raised us up with him and seated us with him in the heavenly places in Christ Jesus, so that in the coming ages he might show the immeasurable riches of his grace in kindness toward us in Christ Jesus. For by grace you have been saved through faith. And this is not your own doing; it is the gift of God, not a result of works, so that no one may boast. For we are his workmanship, created in Christ Jesus for good works, which God prepared beforehand, that we should walk in them. (Ephesians 2:1–10)

Martin Luther King Jr., in his "Letter from a Birmingham Jail" stated,

> There was a time when the church was very powerful in the time when the early Christians rejoiced at being deemed worthy to suffer for what they believed. In those days the church was not merely a thermometer that recorded the ideas and principles of popular opinion; it was a thermostat that transformed society small in number, they were big in commitment. They were too God-intoxicated to be intimidated. By their efforts and example they brought an end to such ancient evils as infanticide and the gladiator games. Things are different now. And if today's church does not recapture the sacrificial spirit of the early church, it will lose its authenticity, forfeit the loyalty of missions, and be dismissed as an irrelevant social club with no meaning for the twentieth century. Every day I meet young people who disappointment with the church has turned into outright disgust.[93]

When it comes to living on mission, we have discussed the importance of being intentional, listening to people and engaging in conversation with them, showing them love, compassion, and fellowship. All these components are very important, but I believe the most important component we can do to really live on mission and love others is by being truthful with them. Yes, we must show them love and compassion; we must serve them, but we must also be truthful. We must do all. Tim Keller stated,

> It is unthinkable that we could truly love an individual and not want both to share the gospel

---

[93] Martin Luther King Jr., "Letter From a Birmingham Jail", in Milestone Documents in African American History by Paul Murray (Armenia, NY: Salem Press, 2017).

EXPERIENCING JESUS THROUGH THE EYES OF THE SAMARITAN WOMAN

> as well as to meet the person's basic needs. Word and deed are the proverbial 'two wings of the airplane.' Which wing is more important? If you love a person, you recognize your friend's most fundamental need is reconciliation to God. But you do not care for his illness or feed him just as a means to an end. You tend to your friend, because you love him.[94]

Thus far in this story, we have seen how Jesus was intentional as He engaged the Samaritan woman; He listened and talked to her, He showed her love and compassion, and He fellowshipped with her. But here is something we really need to understand. Notice Jesus did not just do all these things and then walk away. Now if Jesus had just walked away at this point, she would have considered Him a nice guy who seemed to want to talk to her and get to know her. But Jesus Jesus did not just talk to her, fellowship with her, and show her love and compassion. No! Jesus also moved the conversation to a deeper level and spoke truth into her life, and by doing this, we will soon see where this woman's life was radically changed because of Him revealing the truth into her life. Why is this important? When it comes to living on mission, if we are not careful we can many times engage with someone, talk to them, serve them, fellowship with them, and even show them love and compassion; but then it stops there. For whatever reason, we do not take it any further. It could be because we feel we do not need to take it any further, we could be scared to take it any further or we may not know how to take it further. The truth is that if we want to truly live on mission, we must engage with people with the desire and the willingness to take it to a deeper conversation. I have always said that if all we do is serve someone but never share the gospel with them, then we are just holding their hand and making their life comfortable while they are on their way to hell for eternity. I know this may sound harsh, but I believe it is the truth.

---

[94] Tim Keller, *Ministries of Mercy*, 3rd ed. (Phillipsburg, NJ, P&R Publishing, 2015), 117.

You might be thinking and saying as you read this, "Wait a minute, Patrick, up to this point, you have been saying we need to be engaging people in all these different ways, and now are you telling us these are not worth it?" No, not at all. When it comes to living on mission, yes, we need to be involved in all these ways. We need to be intentional, we need to engage in conversation with people, we need to fellowship with them, and we need to show them love and compassion; but if we never engage them with the truth, then we are missing it. It would the same thing if the offense of a football team huddle up, called the play, ran up to the line of scrimmage, and then instead of running the play, they ran back to the sidelines. Yes, they are to huddled up. Yes, they are to call the play. Yes, they are to go to the line, but they are to also run the play. If they do not, they are missing it.

I would even say we are not fully and truly loving people if we do not share the truth with them. As we engage with people, yes, we want them to be authentic relationships, but the ultimate hope is that we have the opportunity to speak truth in their life. Our relationships do not need to be based on only if they accept the truth, but the hope and the desire is to be open to them and share with them the truth. When I was sharing the truth with my friend, I told him my friendship was not based on if He believed the truth and that I would care about and love him no matter what, but I did still share the truth with him. Again, I think truly showing love and compassion to someone is telling them the truth.

I was listening to a video interview from Penn Fraser Jillette, and in his video, he talks about how he was finishing up a show one night, and he was talking to some people when a guy, who was a Christian, came up to him and shared the gospel with him.[95] Jillette stated in his interview how even though he did not believe because he is an atheist, he respected the guy because he shared what he believed was the truth. Jillette goes on to say something very interesting in the video. He says that if Christians really believe the gospel and how Jesus is the only way to salvation, and if you do not put your faith

---

[95] Jillette, Penn. "A Gift of a Bible." https://youtu.be/6md638smQd8.

EXPERIENCING JESUS THROUGH THE EYES OF THE SAMARITAN WOMAN

in Jesus, you will spend eternity in hell. Jillette says that if Christians believe this, then how can they say they love people if they do not share this truth with them? Jillette actually says, "How much do you have to hate someone to not tell them what you believe is the truth?" I do not know if I would say I agree with him saying how much do you have to hate someone, but I would agree with Jillette in that if we truly say we love and truly want to love people, then how can we not share the truth with them.

Jesus did this with many people He met during His ministry, and we also see Jesus do this with the Samaritan woman. How did He do this? Let's see what He does. As Jesus engaged this woman, remember He started with a general conversation. He started off asking her for a drink of water. As Jesus is talking to her about water, He starts to move the conversation from a general conversation to a deeper, spiritual conversation. First, Jesus was truthful about her sinful life. In verse 16, Jesus says to her, "Go, call your husband, and come here." The woman responds in verse 17, "I have no husband." Jesus then says, "You are right in saying, I have no husband; For you have had five husbands, and the one you now have is not your husband." The woman says, "What you have said is true." Jesus pointed out this woman's sin. We do not know a lot of details about this woman's past, but it seems this woman was involved with sexual immorality. This woman has had five husbands, and now she is apparently living with a man that is not her husband. As Jesus points out her sin, she acknowledges that Jesus is correct. In verse 19, the woman states, "Sir, I perceive that you are a prophet." This woman admits her sin to Jesus and Jesus is calling her to repent of her sins. Matt Carter and Josh Wredburg stated, "Until this woman understands the depth of her sin, she will not long for the salvation Jesus offers."[96]

The truth is that, yes, Jesus was loving and compassionate, but He was also truthful. Jesus did not give her a partial gospel. A gospel that says Jesus loves you for who you are and you do not have to

---

[96] Matt Carter and Josh Wredburg, *Christ-Centered Exposition: John* (Nashville, TN: B&H Publishing, 2017), 97.

change. Yes, anyone can come to Jesus, and yes, Jesus meets us where we are, but the moment we truly meet Jesus, our lives are never the same. Our lives are radically different. The gospel meets you where you are, but it does not leave you where you are. The gospel gives you a new life with new desires, and you are never the same.

As we seek to live on mission and engage people with the gospel, we must be loving and compassionate toward people, but we must be truthful. We must preach a complete gospel that commands confession and repentance of sin. As we engage people with the gospel, if we are not truthful about sin, then we are not preaching the true gospel. Paul says in Galatians 1:8, "But even if we or an angel from heaven should preach to you a gospel contrary to the one we preached to you, let him be accursed. As we have said before, so now I say again: if anyone is preaching to you a gospel contrary to the one you received, let him be accursed." Matt Carter and Josh Wredberg stated, "The gospel without sin is no gospel at all. Yet around the world a sinless, condemnation-free message is being held out as the Christian message."[97]

We must speak the truth about sin. The truth is that when God created the world and part of His creation was man (Genesis 1–2). When God created man, He put them in a garden, and they had a relationship with Him, and there was no sin in the world. Adam and Eve rebelled against God (Genesis 3), and they brought sin into the world. "Therefore, just as sin came into the world through one man, and death through sin, and so death spread to all men because all sinned" (Romans 5:12). The world we currently live in is a broken world full of evil and destruction, and it's not the world God created. Sin causes us to rebel against God, and instead of worshipping Him, we worship ourselves.

Paul tells us in Romans 1:18–25:

> For the wrath of God is revealed from heaven against all ungodliness and unrighteousness of men, who by their unrighteousness sup-

---

[97] Ibid.

> press the truth. For what can be known about God is plain to them, because God has shown it to them. For his invisible attributes, namely, his eternal power and divine nature, have been clearly perceived, ever since the creation of the world, in the things that have been made. So they are without excuse. For although they knew God, they did not honor him as God or give thanks to him, but they became futile in their thinking, and their foolish hearts were darkened. Claiming to be wise, they became fools, and exchanged the glory of the immortal God for images resembling mortal man and birds and animals and creeping things. Therefore God gave them up in the lusts of their hearts to impurity, to the dishonoring of their bodies among themselves, because they exchanged the truth about God for a lie and worshiped and served the creature rather than the Creator, who is blessed forever!

Because of sin, man is always seeking something other than God to bring us joy and satisfaction. Because of sin, instead of pleasing God and living the way God desires us to live, man lives the way he wants to live. Because of sin, man is always rebelling against God and seeking our own pleasure and living in a way that seems right to man.

> In those days there was no king in Israel. Everyone did what was right in his own eyes. (Judges 21:25)

> There is a way that seems right to a man, but its end is the way to death. (Proverbs 14:12)

We see this in our culture today. Our culture today screams loudly that we can live the way we want to, and we do not need God telling us what we can or cannot do, and we do not need a "book" telling us what we can and cannot do. The culture is running faster and faster from God and doing everything it can do to prove there is no God because if you can prove there is no god, then there is no moral way to live, and so we can live anyway we want to because there are no consequences' promotes sexual immorality, such as adultery, homosexuality, nonmarital sex, transgenderism. Not only promotes but also celebrates them. The culture sets aside a whole month to celebrate this. The culture today promotes and celebrates same-sex marriage to the point of tearing down the traditional family. The culture today almost forces, celebrates, and promotes people and children to have sex reassignment operations but, at the same time, shames people if they decide another option or decides they want to change back. The culture today is trying everything they can do to keep parents, churches, and other organizations from talking children out of having sex reassignment operations and also doing everything they can do to stop people from changing their mind or wanting to reverse their decision.

The culture says get married, have fun, but once the fun runs out, just get a divorce. The culture says have as much sex as you want, and if you get pregnant, just have an abortion. The culture says if the current state you live in will not let you have an abortion, we will pay for your travel to a state that will allow you to. We are living in a world where businesses have come out and said they will pay for people to travel to another state to have an abortion, but at the same time, those companies will not pay for people to adopt a child. The world tries to do everything they can to promote and celebrate abortions and, at the same time, will do everything they can to hide and shame adoption. We are living in a world where we will throw billions of dollars at an organization like Planned Parenthood that promotes abortion but, at the same time, trying to shut down pregnancy centers because they give women another option other than abortion.

We also have seen the culture infiltrate into the church. When I was working for Powerade, I was visiting the University of Massachusetts, and on my break, I decided to visit Northampton and go see Jonathan Edwards and the church he pastored. As I arrived,

EXPERIENCING JESUS THROUGH THE EYES OF THE SAMARITAN WOMAN

I noticed they had a sign that stated that all were welcome, which means they welcomed anyone regardless of who they are or whatever their lifestyle was. Now this sounds nice, and yes, churches should welcome anyone, but this church was saying all are welcome, and you can come as you are without changing because Jesus loves all people no matter who you are or what you have done; and you do not have to change. Churches like this are quickly filling up because everyone loves a Jesus who loves, but no one wants a Jesus who judges, calls out sin or says you must repent of your sins. Start preaching this in these churches and see how fast people flee.

If the church is not careful, we can desire people to come to Jesus so much that we preach a partial or attractive gospel that only preaches the love and acceptance of Jesus, but the truth is that this, according to Paul, is no gospel at all. This is a false gospel because it is deceiving to people and really not loving at all. These people are flocking to Jesus because of this message, and one day, if they are not told the truth about sin, they will die thinking they are saved only to find out they are not and will spend eternity in hell.

> Not everyone who says to me, "Lord, Lord," will enter the kingdom of heaven, but the one who does the will of the Father who is in heaven. On that day many will say to me, "Lord, Lord, did we not prophesy in your name, and cast out demons in your name, and do many mighty works in your name?" And then will I declare to them, "I never knew you; depart from me, you worker of lawlessness." (Matthew 7:21–23)

The truth is we must be loving and compassionate, and the best way we can be loving and compassionate is to be truthful. How unloving are Christians if we know the truth and keep it to ourselves and do not share it with the culture?

As we live on mission, we must engage the culture with the truth. Christians must stand against anything that goes against God's Word. God created the world, and He knows how best His creation works. God desires to have a relationship with man, and He wants what is best for man so He has given us His word to know Him and to know how to live a life that leads to human flourishing. If we truly believe this, then we must stand up for this truth, and we must stand against anything that goes against God's Word because we believe going against God's Word leads to destruction both personally and in the society, but if we live a life that lines up with God's Word, this will lead to a life of flourishing, both personally and in the society.

Back in chapter 1, we saw where this woman represented numerous problems that are going on in the world today. Problems such as divorce, sexually immorality, racism, materialism, and false worship. The rest of this chapter will focus on these issues and how we are to speak into these truths according to God's Word. Keep in mind, this book will also not exhaust these topics but will give a general overview of each of these issues.

Divorce

"Jesus said to her, 'Go, call your husband, and come here.' The woman answered him, 'I have no husband.' Jesus said to her, 'You are in saying, I have no husband; for you have had five husbands and the one you now have is not your husband'" (John 4:16–18). Jesus was truthful to the woman about divorce. This woman had been divorced, and Jesus spoke truth into her life. Christians must stand up for God's design for marriage and stand against anything that is outside God's will. This means we must stand against divorce. When God designed marriage, He designed marriage to be permanent. In Genesis 1–2, God created Adam, but God realized how Adam did not have a companion and helper so God created Eve out of Adam as his companion and helper. In Genesis 2:24, God said, "Therefore a man shall leave his father and mother and hold fast to his wife." In Mark 10, some Pharisees come to Jesus and question him about divorce. Jesus says in verse 6, "But from the beginning of creation, God made them male and female. Therefore a man shall leave his father and mother and hold fast to his wife, and the two shall become one flesh. So they are no longer two but one flesh. What therefore

God has joined together, let not man separate." Jesus made it very clear how God always intended marriage to be for life and to never be separated. God hates divorce and never intended it. "For the man who does not love his wife but divorces her, says the Lord, the God of Israel, covers his garment with violence, says the Lord of hosts. So guard yourselves in your spirit, and do not be faithless" (Malachi 2:16).

Sexual Immorality

In John 4:18, Jesus revealed to this woman that she was living with a man whom she is not married to. This woman seemed to be involved in sexual immorality, and Jesus spoke truth about it to her. Christians are to stand against anything that is outside God's design for sex, and we are to stand up for sexual purity. "Therefore a man shall leave his father and his mother and hold fast to his wife, and they shall become one flesh. And the man and his wife were both naked and were not ashamed" (Genesis 2:24). When God created sex, He created sex as a gift that would be shared between a married man and a married woman. This is God's design for sex, and when anyone and society as a whole use sex outside God's design, this leads to destruction both personally and in the society. Our current culture is sex-crazed. Sex is considered and treated like a god. The current culture says we can have sex with whoever we want and whenever we want, and there are no consequences. As Christians, we know this is not the truth, so we must speak up and stand for the truth. If we truly love people, then we must share this truth with them.

Uplifting Education is an organization that seeks to nourish the heart and equip the youth to live fulfilling and meaningful lives. This is what their website stated about the sexual revolution.

> Thanks to the entertainment industry, which has become the primary agent for promoting the values of the sexual revolution throughout the world, young people are growing up in a highly sexualized environment. Every day they

> are bombarded by sexual messages via TV, movies, videos, advertisements (especially on the internet), books, magazines, and music, most of which promote the physical pleasures of sex and downplay any element of responsibility. Premarital and extramarital sexual relations are depicted as glamorous, exciting, and generally without negative consequences. Young people are being fed a never-ending diet of unrealistic portrayals of the sexual experience.[98]

They go on to show the damages of the sexual revolution.

> The psychological and emotional scars resulting from uncommitted sexual relationships precipitate anxiety, low self-esteem, suicidal tendencies, divorce, and family breakdown. Sexually transmitted diseases, including AIDS, and unwanted pregnancies raise concerns about public health and welfare.[99]

This means that we must stand against any sexual immorality. This includes adultery (Exodus 20:14), sex outside marriage (Genesis 2:24), and homosexuality (Romans 1:26–27). "Or do you not know that the unrighteous will not inherit the kingdom of God? Do not be deceived: neither the sexually immoral, nor idolaters, nor adulterers, nor men who practice homosexuality" (1 Corinthians 6:9).

When God created marriage, He created marriage between male and female, and when He created sex, He created sex between a married man and woman. We see this in Genesis 1:27–28 and also in Genesis 2:24. This is the design God has given us and has laid them out in His Word. The truth is that sexual sin is any sex that happens

---

[98] Uplifting Education website, https://www.upliftingeducation.com/consequences-of-the-sexual-revolution.
[99] Ibid.

outside God's design. This means adultery. "You shall not commit adultery" (Exodus 20:14). Jesus tells us in Matthew 5:27–28, "You have heard that it was said, 'you shall not commit adultery. But I say to you that everyone who looks at a woman with lustful intent has already committed with her in his heart." And in Proverbs 6:32, "He who commits adultery lacks sense: he who does it destroys himself." Hebrews 13:4 "Let marriage be held in honor among all, and let the marriage bed be undefiled, for God will judge the sexually immoral and adulterous."

This means sex outside marriage. When God created sex, his design was for it to be between a married man and a married woman (Genesis 2:24).

> Do you not know that your bodies are members of Christ? Shall I then take the members of Christ and make them a members of a prostitute? Never! Or do you not know that he who is joined to a prostitute becomes one body with her? For, as it is written, 'the two will become one flesh. But he who is joined to the Lord becomes one spirit with him. Flee from sexual immorality. Every other sin a person commits is outside the body, but the sexually immoral person sins against his own body. (1 Corinthians 6:15–18)

Paul states in 1 Corinthians 7:9–10, "To the unmarried and the widows I say that it is good for them to remain single, as I am. But if they cannot exercise self-control, they should marry. For it is better to marry than to burn with passion."

This means homosexuality. "You shall not lie with a male as with a woman; it is an abomination" (Leviticus 18:22). Some people argue that this was the God of the Old Testament, and Jesus had a different thought. Some people state that Jesus never condemned homosexuality, but I think He did. How? In Matthew 19, the Pharisees asked Jesus about divorce and in verses 4–6, and Jesus said, "Have you not read that he who created them from the beginning made them male and female, and said, 'Therefore a man shall leave his father and his mother and hold fast to his wife, and the two shall become one flesh'? So they are no longer two but one flesh." Notice what Jesus did? He affirmed Genesis 1:27–28 and Genesis 2:8, which was God's design for marriage. By doing this, Jesus not only defined marriage but He also defined what marriage is not. Think about this: if I took five women and stood them side by side and then pointed to the one who was my wife, not only have I identified who my wife is but also who is not my wife. I believe this is what Jesus did.

Human Life

"A woman from Samaria came to draw water. Jesus said to her, 'Give me a drink.' The Samaritan woman said to him, 'How is it that you, a Jew, ask for a drink from me, a woman of Samaria' (For Jews have no dealings with Samaritans)" (John 4:7–9). This woman was shocked that a male Jew would speak to a female Samaritan. The Jews hated Samaritans and thought of them as less and having no value. By Jesus engaging with this woman, He showed her value. He showed her He cared about her as a human being made in the image of God. Christians must stand against any devaluing of human life. Christians must stand up for life from the womb to the tomb because God values human life. Why does God value human life? God is life, and He is the giver of life. "Then the Lord God formed the man of dust from the ground and breathed into his nostrils the breath of life, and the man became a living creature" (Genesis 2:7). "In his hand is the life of every living thing and the breath of all mankind" (Job 12:10). When God created the world, including humans, He gave life to it all because He is life and He is the giver of life. God made man in His own image.

> So God created man in his own image, in the image of God he created him; male and female he created them. And God blessed them. And God said to them, be fruitful and multiply and fill the earth and subdue it, and have domin-

ion over the fish of the sea and over the birds of the heavens and over every living thing that moves on the earth. (Genesis 1:27–28)

God's most prized creation is humans. When He created us, He created us in His image. He also created humans for a purpose. We were to multiply and fill the earth with His image and His glory. God created humans to have a relationship with Himself. "And the Lord God planted a garden in Eden, in the east, and there he put man whom he had formed" (Genesis 2:8). Genesis 3:8 reveals to us that when God created Adam and Eve and He put them into the garden, He would come to them and spend time with them. God loves us, and He desires to have a relationship with us. He created us to have a relationship with Himself. As Christians, we must stand against any attempt for anyone other than God to take life. God is the only one who can give life, and He should be the only one who can take life. So Christians must stand against murder, euthanasia, suicide, terrorism, and Christian persecution. But just as Christians are to stand against any taking of life, we must also stand up and protect life.

Christians must stand against abortion and stand up for the unborn. Even though Roe vs. Wade was overturned and we can celebrate this, there is still work to be done. The church must continue to stand for the unborn. We have seen videos of Planned Parenthood bragging about taking the body parts and then selling them. We have seen different states fighting for later and later stages of abortion, to the point to where they make it okay to allow a fetus to lie on the table and restrict life support and allow that baby to die. We have seen where the world wants to destroy pregnancy centers. Why? Because they show women different options other than abortion. I think it is funny how they call it pro-choice, but when you really think about it, they only promote one choice, and that is abortion.

As Christians, we must stand up for the unborn because God values life and that fetus is a real baby that God has created. How do we know that fetus is a real human created by God? Because God says it is in His Word.

> Before I formed you in the womb I knew you, before you were born I set you apart; I appointed you as a prophet to the nations. (Jeremiah 1:5)

> For you formed my inward parts; you knitted me together in my mother's womb. I praise you, for I am fearfully and wonderfully made. Wonderful are your works; my soul knows it very well. My frame was not hidden from you, when I was being made in secret, intricately woven in the depths of the earth. Your eyes saw my unformed substance; in your book were written, every one of them, the days that were formed for me, when as yet there was none of them. (Psalm 139:13–16)

> And when Elizabeth heard the greeting of Mary, the baby leaped in her womb. And Elizabeth was filled with the Holy Spirit, and she exclaimed with a loud cry, "Blessed are you among women, and blessed is the fruit of your womb! And why is this granted to me that the mother of my Lord should come to me? For behold, when the sound of your greeting came to my ears, the baby in my womb leaped for joy." (Luke 1:41–44)

Have you ever thought about the first person to recognize the Messiah was the unborn? The word *baby*. The Greek word is *brefos*, which is the same word used for Jesus in the manger. According to God's Word, the baby inside the womb is the same baby as outside the womb. The truth is that we, as Christians, must stand up and speak out for the unborn because they are real human beings who are created in the image of God just like you and me, and as Christians, we are to always protect the sanctity of life.

EXPERIENCING JESUS THROUGH THE EYES OF THE SAMARITAN WOMAN

Christians must stand against any form of racism. In the heart of the civil rights movement, Martin Luther King Jr. led it based on two reasons. First, the Bible reveals the truth that God created all men in His image and all men are equal. Second, the US Constitution stated that all men were equal. When Martin Luther read the Bible and the Constitution, he did not see a country that was living out the truth that "all men are created in the image of God and are all equal." Martin Luther did not see a world of racial harmony and love, but instead, he saw a world of racial division and hate, and he knew this was antithetical to the world God created.

We live in a world that has a long history of racism. We see this in the New Testament with Jews and Gentiles. We see this in all of human history, such as the Holocaust or the Civil Rights Movement. We live in a country that has dealt with racism, and I believe we still see racism even today in this country. As the church, we must not stand for any type of hate and division in this world, but we should always stand for justice and righteousness no matter the cost because that is what God has called us to as His church.

When it comes to standing against racism, here are two biblical truths we can stand on. First, God created all humans in His image, and all humans are equal in God's eyes. We are created in the *imago dei*, which means in the image of God. DA Horton stated, "All people, of every ethnicity, gender, and social class, have the dignity of an image bearer and are therefore due equal respect."[100] Second, when God created man, He created man to love and worship Him, and He also created man to fellowship and love each other; but the problem is that sin has caused man to rebel and hate God and to hate each other. Because of sin, instead of living in peace and harmony with each other, humans would live in a fallen world characterized by hate and division. The truth about sin is that it causes hate and division. Because of sin, man hates God, and man hates man. God created man to live in community with each other with a shared love for God and each other, but sin has caused this community to be destroyed.

---

[100] DA Horton. *Intensional: Kingdom Ethnicity in a Divided World* (Colorado Springs, CO: NAVPress, 2019), 37.

When we look at the world today and see hatred and division among each other, we need to be reminded this is not the world that God created. Jarvis Williams stated, "Sin is the fundamental reason that human beings need to be reconciled first to God and second to one another, for sin has shattered the relationship of human beings with God and one another."[101] This shattered relationship from God and each other is the root of racism. The world states that the reason for racism is social or cultural, but we need to understand the truth is that it is spiritual.

Materialism

"Jesus said to her, 'Everyone who drinks of this water will be thirsty again, but whoever drinks of the water I give will never be thirsty again" (John 4:13–14). This woman was relying her happiness on things of the world, and Jesus told her that these things will never bring her ultimate satisfaction and happiness. She could continue to seek these things, and no matter how much she consumes them, she will never reach true and ultimate happiness. This is like drinking the water in the ocean. Because of the salt, you can continue to drink and you will drink and drink and will never be quenched, and soon you will die from consuming too much water. I remember one time in my life I became obsessed with clothes. I can remember always wanting more and more clothes. I can remember thinking if I just had those jeans or that shirt or those shoes, then I would be happy. I would purchase them and that happiness never came. Sure, I would be happy at first, but that happiness never stayed. It was not long before I would see more clothes and those thoughts would start over, and this was a continual cycle that never ended. My obsession caused problems in my marriage and almost brought us into severe debt issues. It was slowly destroying me personally and my family.

As Christians, we must speak about the truth of materialism. The truth is when God created humans, He created us to have a

---

[101] Jarvis Williams. *One New Man: The Cross and Racial Reconciliation in Pauline Theology* (Nashville, TN: B&H Publishing, 2010), 24.

relationship with Him. Man was to rely on God to ultimately bring him ultimate joy and satisfaction, but sin cased us to rebel against God and to run from God and to seek other things for our joy and satisfaction. Man replaced God with things to bring us the joy and happiness that only God can bring. Paul tells us in Romans 1 that we were created to worship God, but we have replaced God and worshipped the creation instead of the Creator. The truth is only God can truly bring us satisfaction, joy, happiness, and peace. This is what Jesus told the Samaritan woman. He said, "You can continue to drink and drink from this water and will never be quenched." This woman was seeking other things, like sex, for her joy, happiness, and satisfaction; and Jesus told her they will never bring her these things. Only God can. These things will not only not bring us ultimate joy and satisfaction, but they will also lead us to destruction.

False Worship

"Our fathers worshiped on this mountain, but you say that in Jerusalem is the place where people ought to worship." Jesus said to her, "Woman, believe me, the hour is coming when neither on this mountain nor in Jerusalem will you worship the Father." You worship what you do not know, for salvation is of the Jews. But the hour is coming and is now here, when the true worshiper will worship the Father in spirit and truth. God is spirit, and those who worship him must worship in spirit and truth. (John 4:20–24)

This woman was a Samaritan. The Jews worshipped in the Jerusalem temple, and the Samaritans worshipped on Mt. Gerizim. This woman believed the faith of her fathers and her temple worship was all she needed, but Jesus shared a different truth. Carter and Wredburg stated, "She was hoping her religious experience would be enough. She was trusting in the obedience to her fathers."[102] Jesus shared a different truth with her. Jesus shared with her true worship does not come on Mt. Gerizim, and true worship does not even come through the Jewish temple, but true worship comes to the Father through Jesus Christ.

First, Jesus said true worship is in spirit. Worship is a matter of the heart. In Matthew 15:8, Jesus said, "This people honors me with their lips, but their heart is far from me." True worship is not in a place, an object, or a ritual; rather, true worship is from the heart. God is not honored when we are playing church or when we are just going through the motions. He is only honored when we are truly worshiping from all of our being. With all of our heart. Charles Spurgeon stated, "God does not regard our voices, He hears our hearts, and if our hearts do not sing we have not sung at all."[103]

Second, Jesus said true worship is in truth. True worship is centered around God's Word and how He has revealed himself. True worship is when we worship God's way and not our way. Chris Anderson stated, "Worship in truth is biblical worship. It's rooted in the Word of God, not the whims of man. And it's legitimate worship, not contrived. It's true worship, as opposed to fake. It's sincere."[104] John Calvin stated, "If we wish our religion to be approved by God, it must rest on knowledge obtained from His Word."[105]

The truth is God desires His people to worship Him. He created us to worship Him. God also desires the nations to worship Him. John Piper stated, "Missions exist because worship does not. Worship is ultimate, not missions, because God is ultimate, not man. When this age is over, and the countless millions of the redeemed fall

---

[102] Matt Carter and Josh Wredburg, *Christ-Centered Exposition: John* (Nashville, TN: B&H Publishing, 2017), 100.

[103] Kent Hughes, *Preaching the Word: John* (Wheaton, IL: Crossway, 1999), 122.

[104] Chris Anderson, *The God Who Satisfies: How Jesus Seeks, Saves, and Satisfies Samaritan Women Like Us* (Church Works, 2016), 122.

[105] John Calvin, Commentary on the Gospel According to John, vol. 1 (Grand Rapids, MI: Baker Books, 1999), 161.

EXPERIENCING JESUS THROUGH THE EYES OF THE SAMARITAN WOMAN

on their faces before the throne of God, missions will be no more."[106] God desires the nations to worship Him so much He sends His people to the nations to make Himself known. This is why we go to our neighbors, and this is why we go to the nations, so they can know God and worship for what He has done for us through Jesus. We see God's heart for the nations all through Scripture.

> God tells Abraham that through him all the nations will be blessed. (Genesis 12:3)

> So that all the peoples of the earth may know that the Lord is God and that there is no other. (1 Kings 8:60)

> Declare his glory among the nations, his marvelous deeds among all peoples. (1 Chronicles 16:24)

> And he made from one man every nation of mankind to live on all the face of the earth, having determined allotted periods and the boundaries of their dwelling places, that they should seek God and perhaps feel their way towards him and find him. (Acts 17)

As Christians, we must speak the truth about God's salvation that can only come through a relationship with Jesus Christ. True salvation through Jesus Christ is the only way we can attain true worship. Carter and Wredburg stated,

> True salvation makes people worshipers of God. Jesus is basically saying I have come to bring salvation. To worship in spirit and truth

---

[106] John Piper, *Let the Nations Be Glad: The Supremacy of God in Missions* (Grand Rapids, MI: Baker Academic, 2022), 3.

> means that people have turned from self-worship-vowing allegiance to their own efforts and own desires and own glory-and have knelt in obedience and allegiance to the one true God. The only way people turn from self-worship to God worship, from rebellion to obedience, is by embracing the truth about me and receiving the Holy Spirit. This is the salvation I bring.[107]

As Christians, we must speak the truth about sin. The world will tell you you are great just the way you are, but the Bible gives us a different picture. Carter and Wredburg stated, "The Bible describes you as dead, estranged, blind, sick and enslaved. Any message that ignores the reality of human sin is a lie. Just like the woman at the well, we are all sinners."[108] If we do not understand the truth about sin, then we will never understand the truth of the gospel and how we need a savior. Sin is like cancer in that it slowly destroys us from the inside, but the good news is that there is hope. There is hope in the gospel of Jesus Christ.

We must speak the truth of the gospel.

> A woman from Samaria came to draw water. Jesus said to her, "Give me a drink."... The Samaritan woman said to him, "How is it that you, a Jew, ask for a drink from me, a woman of Samaria?"... Jesus answered, "If you knew the gift of God, and who it is that is saying to you, 'Give me a drink,' you would have asked him and he would have given you living water." The woman said to him, "Sir you have nothing to draw water with, and the well is deep. Where do you get that living water? Are you greater than our father

---

[107] Matt Carter and Josh Wredburg, *Christ-Centered Exposition: John* (Nashville, TN: B&H Publishing, 2017), 100.
[108] Ibid., 97.

EXPERIENCING JESUS THROUGH THE EYES OF THE SAMARITAN WOMAN

> Jacob? He gave us the well and drank from it himself, as did his sons and his livestock." Jesus said to her, "Everyone who drinks of this water will be thirsty again, but whoever drinks of the water that I give him will never be thirsty again. The water that I will give him will become in him a spring of water welling up to eternal life." The woman said to him, "Sir, give me this water, so that I will not be thirsty or have to come here to draw water." (John 4:7–15)

As Jesus engaged this woman, He shared the truth with her. This woman was seeking other things to satisfy herself, and Jesus truthfully told her how she can continue to seek these things for her satisfaction and her hope, but only Jesus can truly satisfy us and bring us joy and peace and hope. Jesus wanted this woman to understand He is the only one who can truly save us. Carter and Wredburg stated, "Salvation from her sin was only possible as she came to a right understanding of Jesus Christ. She needed to understand He was the Messiah-the one sent by God to rescue people from sin. No man or woman can be saved apart from Jesus Christ. He is the only way of salvation (John 14:6)."[109] Jesus is the only one who can give us life, both life now and for eternity.

As we engage the world, we must share the truth of the gospel. We must share the truth that only Jesus can save us, satisfy us and give us peace, hope and life. John Piper stated, "The deepest and most enduring happiness is found only in God. Not from God, but in God."[110] We must speak truth to people about how the world we currently live in is full of evil, wickedness, and confusion; this is not the world God made. When God created the world, there was no sin in the world, but when Adam and Eve rebelled against God and sinned against God, they brought sin into the world and turned

---

[109] Matt Carter and Josh Wredburg, *Christ-Centered Exposition: John* (Nashville, TN: B&H Publishing, 2017), 98.
[110] John Piper, *Desiring God* (Sisters, OR: Multnomah Publishers, 2003), 28.

God's world upside down. The good news of the gospel is God did not leave us in our sins, but He sent His Son Jesus to die on the cross for our sins so we can be saved from our sins, forgiven of our sins, and freed from our sins. Because of Jesus, we can experience true happiness, peace, hope, and life. Jesus is the only way. In John 14:6, Jesus said, "I am the way, the truth and the life and no one comes to the Father except through me." And in Acts 4:12 it is said, "And there is salvation in no one else, for there is no other name under the heaven given among men by which we must be saved." If we confess our sins, repent of our sins, and surrender our lives to Jesus, we can experience salvation. We can be reconciled back to a relationship with God and be with Him and live with Him forever.

As we engage the world, we need to show the world how the gospel is the answer to a lost and dying world. The world is broken and is longing for and seeking hope, peace, happiness, and satisfaction, but the world is looking for it in the wrong place. The world seeks these things through alcohol, drugs, sex, money, and power, and, like Jesus said, the world can continue to seek these things through these means, and it will never find what it is looking. It will continue to drink these waters and their thirst will never be quenched. Only Jesus can quench our thirst and bring us true hope, peace, happiness, and satisfaction. The world will tell you have as much sex as you want in your life and that will bring you happiness, but it does not. The world will tell you to have a good career and make lots of money and that will truly make you happy, but it will not. The world will tell you to just be spiritual and that will make you happy, but it will not. The world will tell you to basically worship yourself and take care of yourself and you will be happy, but you will not. The truth is none of these things will truly make us happy. Only a relationship with Jesus Christ can and will bring you true happiness.

In 2005, Steve Kroft from *60 minutes* sat down with NFL quarterback Tom Brady. In this interview, Tom was talking about his successful career and this is what Tom stated,

> Why do I have three Super Bowl rings, and
> still think there's something greater out there for

EXPERIENCING JESUS THROUGH THE EYES OF THE SAMARITAN WOMAN

me? I mean, maybe a lot of people would say, "Hey man, this is what is." I reached my goal, my dream, my life. Me, I think: God, it's gotta be more than this. I mean this can't be what it's all cracked up to be. I mean I've done it. I'm 27. And what else is there for me."[111]

Kroft then asked, "What's the answer?" Tom then said,

> I wish I knew. I wish I knew. I mean I think that's part of me trying to go out and experience other things. I love playing football, and I love being a quarterback for this team, but, at the same time, I think there's a lot of other parts about me that I'm trying to find. I know what ultimately makes me happy are family and friends, and positive relationships with great people. I think I get more out of that than anything.[112]

Tom Brady is searching for true happiness and true satisfaction, but he is seeking it in the things of the world that will never deliver what he is searching for.

Worshipping the god of this world will never bring you true happiness but will only bring you destruction. Worshipping the one true God will bring you the happiness and the peace and hope you have been looking for and are longing for. In his book *Confessions*, St. Augustine stated, "Our heart is unquiet until it rests in you."[113] Tim Keller stated, "If you are experiencing unquiet and dissatisfaction in

---

[111] Interview with Tom Brady on *60 minutes* in November 5, 2005. https://www.cbsnews.com/news/transcript-tom-brady-part-3/
[112] Ibid.
[113] St. Augustine of Hippo, *The Confessions: With an Introduction and Contemporary Criticism*, ed. David Vincent Meconi (San Francisco, CA: Ignatius, 2012), 3.

your life, they may be signs of a need for God that is there, but which is not recognized as such."[114]

If you are reading this and you do not have a relationship with Christ, maybe you can identify with this in that you have been trying to find peace, happiness, hope, and satisfaction and you have not been able to find. Maybe you are still looking for it. Like this woman, you have been looking for it in the wrong place. The good news is that is not too late. The good news is that no matter what you have done or where you have been or where you currently are, I want you to know that Jesus loves you. He loves you so much that He died on the cross for your sins so that you can be saved, forgiven, and freed from your sins, so that you can have peace, hope, and satisfaction. He loves you so much He died for you so you can be reconciled back to a relationship with God and live with Him now and for eternity.

How can you receive this great news? By confessing your sins to Jesus, repenting of your sins, and asking Jesus to save you. Asking Jesus to come into your life and surrender to Him and allow Him to be the Lord of your life. If you do this, I promise you He will save you. How can I promise you this? Because God has promised you this in His Word:

> And it shall come to pass that everyone who calls on the name of the Lord shall be saved. (Joel 2:32)

> And it shall come to pass that everyone who calls on the name of the Lord shall be saved. (Acts 2:21)

> To him all the prophets bear witness that everyone who believes In him receives forgiveness of sins through his name. (Acts 10:43)

---

[114] Tim Keller, *Making Sense of God: An Invitation to the Skeptical* (New York, NY: Penguin Random House, 2016), 28.

And they said, "Believe in the Lord Jesus and you will be saved, you and your household." (Acts 16:31)

If you confess with your mouth that Jesus is Lord and believe in your heart that God raised him from the dead, you will be saved. (Romans 10:9)

For everyone who calls on the name of the Lord will be saved. (Romans 10:13)

Conclusion

Because Jesus is the only way we can be saved and have peace, hope, satisfaction, and life, this is why Christians must go and take the gospel of Jesus to a lost and dying world. Scripture tells us the only way people will believe is if they hear, and the only way they will hear is if someone preaches, and the only way they will preach is if they are sent (Romans 10:14–15). If people do not hear and they do not believe, then they will spend eternity in hell, but if people go and preach the good news, then people will hear, and they will believe, and they will be saved, and they will spend eternity with Jesus in His kingdom for eternity. This is why we must go, and we must share the good news of the gospel to those who have yet to hear because eternity is at stake.

7

Jesus Changed Her Life

Therefore, if anyone is in Christ, the new creation has come: The old has gone, the new is here! All this is from God, who reconciled us to himself through Christ and gave us the ministry of reconciliation: that God was reconciling the world to himself in Christ, not counting people's sins against them. And he has committed to us the message of reconciliation. We are therefore Christ's ambassadors, as though God were making his appeal through us. We implore you on Christ's behalf: Be reconciled to God. God made him who had no sin to be sin for us, so that in him we might become the righteousness of God. (2 Corinthians 5:17-21, NIV)

I was raised in a Christian home and was saved when I was eleven years old. I remember sharing the gospel with family and friends so I did have fruit in my life, but though high school and through college, I fell far away from God. After graduating from school, I moved to Birmingham, Alabama, and met my future wife. We started dating, and neither one of us were regularly attending church. We Valleydale Church in a phone book and started visiting. We got married, joined Valleydale, and for many years just went to service and that was about

EXPERIENCING JESUS THROUGH THE EYES OF THE SAMARITAN WOMAN

it. I remember one year, we decided together that we were going to read the entire Bible in one year. We were both committed, and we both did it. Little did I know that God was going to use this to radically change my life.

After I finished reading the Bible in a year, I really started craving God's Word. I truly could not get enough of it. I signed up for a two-year certificate program in biblical studies at a Bible college. I finished the program in one year because I just could not study enough of the Bible. I started to get involved in the church; I started serving in the parking lot and this led to leading the parking lot team; to being in and teaching a small group and then starting a small group. At this point, I felt God calling me into ministry, and so I went and talked to the discipleship pastor. He brought me on staff as part-time men's ministry director. I started seminary, and after three years of being a part-time staff at Valleydale, the church hired me as a full-time pastor, where I still am serving today.

I share my story to tell you the truth of how radically God changed my life. I do believe I was saved when I was eleven, but I also believe when God drew me back closer to Him after many years, this experience of Jesus was much more powerful. I truly understand the power of God and how He can radically change your life when you experience Him. When you truly experience Jesus, you will never be the same. He will radically change your life. Trust me, I know from experience!

In this story, as this woman experienced Jesus, her life would never be the same. In John 4:25–26, it states, "The woman said to him, 'I know that Messiah is coming (he who is called Christ). When he comes, he will tell us all thing.' Jesus said to her, 'I who speak to you am he.'" This woman knew about the Messiah, and Jesus then revealed to her that the Messiah that she knew about and had been waiting for was He. The Messiah is right there in her midst. The Messiah is the man who engaged her and asked her for a drink of water. Imagine how this woman may have felt! Have you ever thought how the Savior of the world, the King of the world, the Creator and Sustainer of the world desires to know you, have a relationship with you, and talk to you. Is this not amazing? Does this not blow you away? This woman must have been blown away. John MacArthur stated, "Jesus' words must have rocked the woman to the core of her being. The man who just a few minutes earlier had made a simple request for a drink of water now claimed to be the long-awaited Messiah."[115]

Verse 28 tells us, "So the woman left her water jar and went away into town and said to the people, 'Come, see a man who told me all that I ever did. Can this be the Christ?'" MacArthur stated, "A stranger who knew all about her past was hardly an ordinary man. So profound was Jesus' impact on her that she did not hesitate to share the news about Him-even with those familiar with her sordid reputation."[116] Think about this as we first came on this story; it was revealed this woman would come to get water at the hottest part of the day to avoid the other people in the village. This woman was isolated from her village, but the moment she experienced Jesus, she did not care about this. All she wanted to do was go and tell them all that Jesus told her. The moment she experienced Jesus, all she wanted to do was to share Him with others so they can experience Him as well. This is what experiencing Jesus and tasting the good news of the gospel will do and should do to us.

Chris Anderson stated,

> Her conversion changed everything. She had to share what she learned. News as glorious as the arrival of the Messiah couldn't be hoarded. Like the four lepers in 2 Kings 7:9, her conscience bound to her to share the good news she had learned. In her haste, she left her water jar and ran to town. She had to tell somebody-anybody! everybody! About Jesus.[117]

---

[115] John MacArthur, *The MacArthur New Testament Commentary: John 1–11* (Chicago, IL: Moody Publishers, 2006), 150.
[116] Ibid., 156.
[117] Chris Anderson, *The God Who Satisfies: How Jesus Seeks, Saves, and Satisfies Samaritan Women Like Us* (Church Works, 2016), 148.

EXPERIENCING JESUS THROUGH THE EYES OF THE SAMARITAN WOMAN

Have you ever experienced something so great that all you wanted to do was tell someone? Do you remember that feeling where you just could not wait to tell someone? I remember when I was in school and I would make a good grade and all I wanted to do was go and tell my parents. I remember having to wait till school got out, and it about drove me crazy waiting. This is how this woman must have felt. She was so excited that verse 30 tells us the people went out to see Jesus because of this woman. This is what the gospel does to us. When we truly experience the gospel, we cannot wait to share it with someone. It almost will drive us crazy until we can tell someone. John Calvin stated, "This is the nature of faith, that when we have become partakers of eternal life, we wish to bring others to share with us."[118]

Christians, I want to be truthful here. We have truly complicated evangelism. We have made evangelism out to something where we feel we need a seminary degree before we share. We make it out to feel we need weeks and weeks of evangelism training before we can go and share the gospel with others. Think about this woman. The moment she experienced the gospel, what did she do? Did she immediately sign up for Bible college or seminary? Did she immediately sign up for a six-week evangelism course at her local church? No, not at all. The moment she experienced Jesus, she ran into her village, and she told them all that Jesus did for her.

David Platt, on the *Pray the Word* podcast, stated,

> This woman, this Samaritan woman who meets Jesus at the well, has a conversation with him, discovers that this is the Messiah, the Christ who promises her satisfaction, a spring of water in her soul welling up to eternal life who calls her to worship and spirit and truth she encounters Jesus. That's all she did. She encountered Jesus and immediately she went back into the town.

---

[118] John Calvin, Commentary on the Gospel According to John, vol 1(Grand Rapids, MI: Baker Books, 1999), 149.

> She starts telling everybody about who she has met and says why don't you come out and listen to this man, see this man. This woman became an instant witness about Jesus.[119]

Platt goes on to say,

> Once you encounter Christ, that's all it takes to tell to other people to look to Christ, see who Jesus is, see what Jesus has done. You don't have to go to seminary, you don't have to have a certain amount of training of Bible knowledge, you don't have to have anything but an encounter with Jesus to be equipped to be able to share Jesus with others, to give testimony to Jesus.[120]

The truth is that there are lots of Christians who are sitting around believing, and some may have even been told that they need lots of evangelism training before they share the gospel. There are some Christians who feel they need a seminary degree or at least some level of education before they can share the gospel. But the truth is that all you need is to experience Jesus, and you are equipped to go and tell others what Jesus has done for you. In fact, I believe you already know how to do this.

Let me ask you a question: Have you ever eaten a really good burger? What did you do the moment you were finished eating it? You probably called four or five of your friends and told them how good this burger was. You may have even begged them to go and try it. You may have even offered to take them yourself to get this burger. Now think about this. You do this for a really good burger, but what we are talking about here is the best news in the world. We are talking about something so much greater than a good burger. We are talking about the gospel of Jesus Christ. We are talking about

---

[119] David Platt, "A Testimony Worth Telling: John 4:39," Radical: Pray the Word (August 13, 2019) https://radical.net/podcasts/pray-the-word/a-testimony-worth-telling-john-439/.

[120] Ibid.

true happiness, true peace, true satisfaction and true life. Don't get we wrong, we do need to be able to walk someone through the steps of the gospel, and please do not get me wrong, it's good for churches to train and equip you to share the gospel. I do this at my current church. But ultimately, when it comes to sharing the truth of the gospel, it is really about telling others what Jesus has done for your life and then showing them how Jesus can change their life as well. Platt stated, "An encounter with Jesus is all that is needed to be equipped to testify to the gospel of Jesus Christ."[121] That is all this woman did and this is all we need to do. We have truly complicated evangelism.

Conclusion

The good news of the gospel is that it changes your life. The Samaritan woman experienced Jesus, and her life was radically changed. Her life was never the same. This is what the gospel does. When someone truly experiences Jesus Christ, their life will never be the same. I was on a trip to San Diego to visit some church planters, and one of the church planters named Logan shared an amazing story with us. A few weeks before he launched his new church, he was out into the community meeting people and businesses. He came upon a barber shop where he met a man named Alan. Alan was a nonbeliever who was living with his girlfriend. Logan asked if he could pray for them, and they all said yes. Logan left, and on launch Sunday, Alan and his family showed up to church. Over the next number of months, Logan would meet with Alan, and Alan would ask hard questions. After several months and many conversations, Alan gave his life to Christ. Praise God! Logan told me how radically Alan's life has changed since he met Christ. As I heard this story, I could not help but think this is exactly what the gospel does to people. The gospel amazingly changes your life. Like the Samaritan woman, Alan's life will never be the same since he met Jesus.

---

[121] David Platt, "A Testimony Worth Telling: John 4:39," Radical: Pray the Word (August 13, 2019) https://radical.net/podcasts/pray-the-word/a-testimony-worth-telling-john-439/.

The good news of the gospel also gives us this overwhelming need to share this good news with others. The moment this woman experienced Jesus, she ran into her village and told them all about Him. If you have experienced Jesus, then you know what I am talking about, but if not, imagine getting the best news in the world told to you and experiencing the most amazing thing in your life. How does this make you feel? It makes you personally feel great, but you also greatly want others to know this and experiencing this as well. You go to a great restaurant or watch a great movie or experience something else so great, what do you do? You are so excited you cannot wait till you can go and tell someone this good news so they can experience it.

The truth is that we get this excited over food or a movie, but what I am talking about is the greatest news and greatest experience in the world, so imagine how this would and should make you feel. The truth is that the moment we experience the best thing in the world, which is Jesus Christ, it should overwhelm us with this great burden to go and tell others about Jesus so they can experience Him as well. Think about all the missionaries in the world who have sacrificed greatly for Jesus. People like Adoniram Judson, William Carey, John Paton, Lottie Moon. And many others. Why did they do it? Because they had experienced the good news of the gospel of Jesus Christ, and, because they had experienced Jesus, they had an overwhelming need to go and tell others about this good news, so they can know the truth and experience Jesus as well. When John Paton was burdened to go and take the gospel to the unreached people in the South Seas, he received great resistance from many people. One elder told him, "You will be eaten by cannibals," to which Paton responded, "Mr. Dickson, you are advanced in years now, and your own prospect is soon to be laid in the grave, there to be eaten by worms; I confess to you, that if I can but live and die serving and honoring the Lord Jesus, it will make no difference to me whether I am eaten by cannibals or by worms."[122]

---

[122] John Paton, *John G. Paton: The Autobiography of the Pioneer Missionary to the New Hebrides* (Banner of Truth, 2013), 11–12.

EXPERIENCING JESUS THROUGH THE EYES OF THE SAMARITAN WOMAN

Paton, along with many others, sacrificed greatly to get the gospel to those who had yet to hear. They had experienced the greatness of Jesus, and they wanted to share Jesus with others. They had such a burden to get the gospel to those who had not heard they were willing to sacrifice and suffered greatly for the gospel. This is what the gospel does to us. The gospel should cause us to have such an overwhelming desire and burden to get this good news to those who have not heard and we should want others to know Jesus and experience Him as well. This is why we go, and this is why we sacrifice and suffer for the gospel. This is how great the gospel is.

I believe one of the best stories in the Bible that reveals the power of the gospel is the testimony of the apostle Paul. Paul shares his story in Acts 22:1–16:

> "Brothers and father, hear the defense that I now make before you." And when they heard that he was addressing them in the Hebrew language, they became even more quiet. And he said: "I am a Jew, born in Tarsus in Cilicia, but brought up in this city, educated at the feet of Gamaliel according to the strict manner of the law of our fathers, being zealous for God as all of you are this day. I persecuted this Way to the death, binding and delivering to prison both men and women, as the high priest and the whole council of elders can bear me witness. From them I received letters to the brothers, and I journeyed toward Damascus to take those also who were there and bring them in bonds to Jerusalem to be punished. "As I was on my way and drew near to Damascus, about noon a great light from heaven suddenly shone around me. And I fell to the ground and heard a voice saying to me, 'Saul, Saul, why are you persecuting me?' And I answered, 'Who are you, Lord?' And he said to me, 'I am Jesus of Nazareth, whom you are persecuting.' Now those who were

with me saw the light but did not understand the voice of the one who was speaking to me. And I said, 'What shall I do, Lord?' And the Lord said to me, 'Rise, and go into Damascus, and there you will be told all that is appointed for you to do.' And since I could not see because of the brightness of that light, I was led by the hand by those who were with me, and came into Damascus. And one Ananias, a devout man according to the law, well spoken of by all the Jews who lived there, came to me, and standing by me said to me, 'Brother Saul, receive your sight.' And at that very hour I received my sight and saw him. And he said, 'The God of our fathers appointed you to know his will, to see the Righteous One and to hear a voice from his mouth; for you will be a witness for him to everyone of what you have seen and heard. And now why do you wait? Rise and be baptized and wash away your sins, calling on his name.'"

The apostle Paul was basically a terrorist persecuting the disciples of Jesus. He was on his way to Damascus to persecute more Christians when Jesus came to him, and through his experience with Jesus, he was converted and became a disciple of Jesus. The moment Paul experienced Jesus his life would never be the same. He was radically changed. The moment Paul became a disciple of Jesus, he did everything he could to get the good news of the gospel to those who had not heard.

> So I am eager to preach the gospel to you also who are in Rome. (Romans 1:15)

> I am speaking the truth in Christ-I am not lying; my conscience bears witness in the Holy Spirit-that I have great sorrow and unceasing

anguish in my heart. For I could wish that I myself were accursed and cut off from Christ for the sake of my brothers, my kinsmen according to the flesh. (Romans 9:1–3)

And thus I make it my ambition to preach the gospel, not where Christ has already been named, lest I build on someone's else foundation. (Romans 15:20)

But we preach Christ crucified, a stumbling block to Jews and folly to Gentiles. (1 Corinthians 1:23)

For if I preach the gospel, that gives me no ground for boasting. For necessary is laid upon me. Woe to me if I do not preach the gospel! (1 Corinthians 9:16)

For I decided to know nothing among you except Jesus Christ and him crucified. (1 Corinthians 2:2)

Paul was very passionate about getting the gospel to those who had not heard because he had experienced the greatness of Jesus, and he wanted others to experience Him so he did everything he could to get the gospel to them. When you first meet Paul in Scripture, you see a man doing whatever he can to stop the gospel, and when you last see Paul in Scripture, you see a man doing whatever he can spread the gospel. Paul wanted so desperately to get the gospel to the nations that he was willing to suffer greatly for the gospel. Listen to what Paul says in 2 Corinthians 11:21–28,

But whatever anyone else dares to boast of—I am speaking as a fool—I also dare to boast of that. Are they Hebrews? So am I. Are

> they Israelites? So am I. Are they offspring of Abraham? So am I. Are they servants of Christ? I am a better one—I am talking like a madman—with far greater labors, far more imprisonments, with countless beatings, and often near death. Five times I received at the hands of the Jews the forty lashes less one. Three times I was beaten with rods. Once I was stoned. Three times I was shipwrecked; a night and a day I was adrift at sea; on frequent journeys, in danger from rivers, danger from robbers, danger from my own people, danger from Gentiles, danger in the city, danger in the wilderness, danger at sea, danger from false brothers; in toil and hardship, through many a sleepless night, in hunger and thirst, often without food, in cold and exposure. And, apart from other things, there is the daily pressure on me of my anxiety for all the churches.

And also in Colossians 1:24 is the following: "Now I rejoice in my sufferings for your sake, and in my flesh I am filling up what is lacking in Christ's affliction for the sake of his body, that is, the church." Paul was so passionate about the gospel that he was even willing to die for the gospel.

> For I am already being poured out as a drink offering, and the time of my departure has come. I have fought the good fight, I have finished the race, I have kept the faith. Henceforth there is laid up for me the crown of righteousness, which the Lord, the righteous judge, will award to me on that day, and not only to me but also to all who have loved his appearing. (2 Corinthians 4:6–8)

EXPERIENCING JESUS THROUGH THE EYES OF THE SAMARITAN WOMAN

This is how powerful the gospel is to be able to radically change a man so that he would be willing to suffer and die to get the gospel to those who have yet to here.

As Christians, like Paul, we should be so in love with Jesus that we should have a deep burden for the nations to know and experience Jesus as well. This should cause us to do whatever we can to get the gospel to those who have not heard, and no amount of suffering or sacrifice should stop us. This is the power of the gospel. This is what the gospel should do to us. This is what happens when we experience Jesus.

8

Jesus Shared His Time

> And Jesus came and said to them, "All authority in heaven and on earth has been given to me. Go therefore and make disciples of all nations, baptizing them in the name of the Father and of the Son and of the Holy Spirit, teaching them to observe all that I have commanded you. And behold, I am with you always, to the end of the age." (Matthew 28:18–20)

For the past three years on Monday nights, my wife and I host a college and young professionals discipleship group. This is one of our favorite things to do together. We both love to invest in the next generation by inviting them into our lives and investing in theirs. To be honest, one of my favorite things in ministry is to watch God change someone's life as they spend time in His Word. I love to open up God's Word with them and help them know God more. Basically, I love being a disciple maker.

Jesus not only commanded us to go and make disciples but Jesus was also our great model of a disciple maker.

> Many Samaritans from that town believed in him because of the woman's testimony, "He told me all that I ever did." So when the Samaritans

EXPERIENCING JESUS THROUGH THE EYES OF THE SAMARITAN WOMAN

> came to him, they asked him to stay with them, and he stayed there two days. And many more believed because of his word. They said to the woman, "It is no longer because of what you said that we believe, for we have heard for ourselves, and we know that this is indeed the Savior of the world." (John 4:39–42)

After the Samaritan woman ran into the village and told them about Jesus, many believed from her testimony, and they went to Jesus and asked Him to stay. He stayed for two days and many more believed through His Word. Jesus spent time with them, investing in them and revealing the truth of God's Word. As Jesus spent time with them, many more believed many more believed because of His Word. As we seek to engage people with the gospel of Jesus Christ, we must spend time with them, revealing the truth of God's Word, so they can know Jesus more and, by knowing Him more, their faith will grow stronger. This is the goal of discipleship. Discipleship is investing in someone else's life, revealing the truth of God's Word, watching their faith and their relationship with God grow stronger and deeper, and watching them live out their faith in their lives. Caryn Reeder, in her book *The Samaritan Woman's Story*, stated,

> The Samaritan woman models Christian discipleship. Through her questions and challenges to Jesus, she grows in understanding. She brings her deeds into the light to be seen. She witnesses to Jesus among her neighbors. The Samaritan woman represents John's ideal disciple. Her work as an evangelist sets a precedent for all disciples to follow. Her story should empower woman and men today to seek understanding and to witness to the identity of Jesus.[123]

---

[123] Caryn Reeder, *The Samaritan Woman's Story* (Downers Grove, IL: InterVarsity Press, 2022), 174.

This is a great reminder that the Great Commission tells us to go and make disciples. The verb is to make disciples. This is more than evangelism. Evangelism is a part of it, but it is more than evangelism. The Great Commission does not say to go and make converts; rather, it says, "Go and make disciples." As we go and engage the world with the gospel, yes, we must share the gospel; but we must also invest in their lives, revealing all the truths of God's Word so their faith can grow stronger, and their relationship with God can grow deeper. I have led many men's discipleship groups, and in one particular year, I led a group of Immature believers and it was probably one of my favorite groups I have ever led. When we first started meeting, you could tell they were not really experienced in reading and studying Scripture. Every week, they really did not have a lot of insights from the weekly readings, and they did not have a lot of questions and comments. As we continued week after week, studying one to two chapters in the Bible, over time I saw them grow in their faith, their knowledge of the Bible, and their relationship with God. To be very honest with you, it was awesome to witness God do this in their lives through studying His Word every day. By the end of the year, they were providing great insights every week, asking a lot more question every week, and they were also providing great thoughts and comments every week. It was a joy to spend time with them every week and watch what God did in their lives. To be honest with you, outside my relationship with God and my family, there is nothing better than watching God grow someone in their faith and their relationship with Him. This is the beauty and joy of making disciples.

You may be reading this and saying, "Okay, Patrick, I really want to start making disciples, but I just do not know how. So how do we make disciples?" To answer this, let's look at how Jesus did it. I think He would be a good place to start. You cannot go wrong with Jesus.

> While walking by the Sea of Galilee, he saw
> two brothers, Simon (who is called Peter) and
> Andrew his brother, casting a net into the sea,

EXPERIENCING JESUS THROUGH THE EYES OF THE SAMARITAN WOMAN

> for they were fisherman. And he said to them, "Follow me, and I will make you fishers of men." Immediately they left their nets and followed him. And going on from there he saw two other brothers, James and John, in the boat with Zebedee their father, mending their nets, and he called them. Immediately they left their boat and their father and followed him. (Matthew 4:18–22)

The Greek word for *mending* is *katartizo*, which means "preparing" or "equipping." They were mending the net so it can function properly. Notice these were fishermen who were equipping the net to catch fish, but Jesus would call and equip them to catch people. When Jesus spoke of fishing, His context was not what we think of. It would not be with a fishing pole, but with a net. A net was something you had to have a partner to help with. When Jesus called His disciples to fish for people, His intent was that they do it in teams. The context was relational. Discipleship is about following Jesus while being in fellowship with other believers as they fish for people together. There are three areas of focus: Follow Jesus, fellowship with other believers and fish for people.

First, Jesus focused on their relationship with the Father. He taught them the importance of spending time with God through prayer.

> Now Jesus was praying in a certain place, and when he finished, one of his disciples said to him, "Lord, teach us to pray, as John taught his disciples." And he said to them, "When you pray, say: 'Father, hallowed be your name. Your kingdom come. Give us each day our daily bread, and forgive us our sins, for we ourselves forgive everyone who is indebted to us. And lead us not into temptation.' And he said to them, "Which of you who has a friend will go to him at midnight and say to him, 'Friend, lend me three loaves, for a friend of

mine has arrived on a journey, and I have nothing to set before him'; and he will answer from within, 'Do not bother me; the door is now shut, and my children are with me in bed. I cannot get up and give you anything'? I tell you, though he will not get up and give him anything because he is his friend, yet because of his impudence he will rise and give him whatever he needs. And I tell you, ask, and it will be given to you; seek, and you will find; knock, and it will be opened to you. For everyone who asks receives, and the one who seeks finds, and to the one who knocks it will be opened. What father among you, if his son asks for a fish, will instead of a fish give him a serpent; or if he asks for an egg, will give him a scorpion? If you then, who are evil, know how to give good gifts to your children, how much more will the heavenly Father give the Holy Spirit to those who ask him!" (Luke 11:1–13)

He taught them the importance of spending time with God through His Word.

> "Whoever has my commandments and keeps them, he it is who loves me. And he who loves me will be loved by my Father, and I will love him and manifest myself to him." Judas (not Iscariot) said to him, "Lord, how is it that you will manifest yourself to us, and not to the world?" Jesus answered him, "If anyone loves me, he will keep my word, and my Father will love him, and we will come to him and make our home with him. Whoever does not love me does not keep my words. And the word that you hear is not mine but the Fathers who sent me." (John 14:21–24)

EXPERIENCING JESUS THROUGH THE EYES OF THE SAMARITAN WOMAN

Second, Jesus taught them the importance of a relationship with one another. In John 13:1–15, we see Jesus teaching them the importance of serving one another.

> Now before the Feast of the Passover, when Jesus knew that his hour had come to depart out of this world to the Father, having loved his own who were in the world, he loved them to the end. During supper, when the devil had already put it into the heart of Judas Iscariot, Simon's son, to betray him, Jesus, knowing that the Father had given all things into his hands, and that he had come from God and was going back to God, rose from supper. He laid aside his outer garments, and taking a towel, tied it around his waist. Then he poured water into a basin and began to wash the disciples' feet and to wipe them with the towel that was wrapped around him. He came to Simon Peter, who said to him, "Lord, do you wash my feet?" Jesus answered him, "What I am doing you do not understand now, but afterward you will understand." Peter said to him, "You shall never wash my feet." Jesus answered him, "If I do not wash you, you have no share with me." Simon Peter said to him, "Lord, not my feet only but also my hands and my head!" Jesus said to him, "The one who has bathed does not need to wash, except for his feet, but is completely clean. And you are clean, but not every one of you." For he knew who was to betray him; that was why he said, "Not all of you are clean." When he had washed their feet and put on his outer garments and resumed his place, he said to them, "Do you understand what I have done to you? You call me Teacher and Lord, and you are right, for so I am. If I then, your Lord and Teacher, have washed

> your feet, you also ought to wash one another's feet. For I have given you an example, that you also should do just as I have done to you."

In John 13:34–35, we see Jesus teaching them the importance of loving one another. "A new commandment I give to you, that you love one another: just as I have loved you, you also are to love one another. By this all people will know that you are my disciples, if you have love for one another." Jesus knew that if they loved one another, this would be a great witness of the gospel to the watching world. Unfortunately, we are not doing a good job of this on social media. Every time I go on social media, all I see are Christians arguing and putting other Christians down and pastors putting other pastors down. This is not showing the world the true gospel. I was recently talking to a Christian and he said he has unbelieving friends who see this arguing going on with Christians and are saying they do not want anything to do with Jesus because of how they are seeing Christians treat one another. The world is watching, and we better wake up because God is not being honored by our actions.

Third, Jesus taught them the importance of going and living on mission and making disciples. In Luke 9, Jesus sends out the twelve.

> And he called the twelve together and gave them power and authority over all demons and to cure diseases, and he sent them out to proclaim the kingdom of God and to heal. And he said to them, "Take nothing for your journey, no staff, nor bag, nor bread, nor money; and do not have two tunics. And whatever house you enter, stay there, and from there depart. And wherever they do not receive you, when you leave that town shake off the dust from your feet as a testimony against them." And they departed and went through the villages, preaching the gospel and healing everywhere.

EXPERIENCING JESUS THROUGH THE EYES OF THE SAMARITAN WOMAN

In Luke 10, Jesus sends out the seventy-two.

> After this the Lord appointed seventy-two others and sent them on ahead of him, two by two, into every town and place where he himself was about to go. And he said to them, "The harvest is plentiful, but the laborers are few. Therefore pray earnestly to the Lord of the harvest to send out laborers into his harvest. Go your way; behold, I am sending you out as lambs in the midst of wolves. Carry no moneybag, no knapsack, no sandals, and greet no one on the road. Whatever house you enter, first say, 'Peace be to this house!' And if a son of peace is there, your peace will rest upon him. But if not, it will return to you. And remain in the same house, eating and drinking what they provide, for the laborer deserves his wages. Do not go from house to house. Whenever you enter a town and they receive you, eat what is set before you. Heal the sick in it and say to them, 'The kingdom of God has come near to you.' But whenever you enter a town and they do not receive you, go into its streets and say, 'Even the dust of your town that clings to our feet we wipe off against you. Nevertheless know this, that the kingdom of God has come near.' I tell you, it will be more bearable on that day for Sodom than for that town."

Conclusion

When it comes to living on mission and engaging the world with the gospel, we must engage them, share the truth of the gospel, and disciple them. Remember, the Great Commission commands us to go and make disciples. These were Jesus' last words to us before He went to be with the Father, and so I believe when we meet the Lord someday face-to-face, He will probably not ask us how often we went to church or read our Bibles, how often we served the church, or how often we served the community. He will probably not ask us how many mission trips we went on. These are great things to do, but I believe the one question Jesus will ask us is how many disciples we made. How would you answer this right now? We need to be ready to answer this question.

As we invest in people's lives and disciple them, we need to be reminded and follow the way Jesus did it. We need to teach them and show them the importance of spending time with God and growing in our relationship with Him. We need to teach them and show them the importance of loving and caring for their brother and sisters in Christ. We also need to teach them and show them the importance of living on mission and making disciples of the nations. This is the model Jesus left for us, and we must follow Him as He makes us fishers of men.

9

Conclusion

> How then will they call on him in whom they have not believed? And how are they to believe in him of whom they have never heard? And how are they to hear without someone preaching? And how are they to preach unless they are sent? As it is written, "How beautiful are the feet of those who preach the good news!" (Romans 10:14–15)

These are very powerful and very important words by Paul. If we never send and if we never go and preach and if they never hear then they will never believe. When it comes to the Great Commission, God could have done anything He wanted. He could have spelled out John 3:16 in the clouds. He could have shouted the gospel from the heavens. Even though God could have gotten the gospel out any way He wanted to, He has chosen, in His sovereignty, to send and preach the gospel through His people.

If God's people do not go and proclaim the gospel, people will not hear, and they will not believe and they will spend eternity in hell without Christ. These words in Romans should motivate us to be obedient and go and proclaim the gospel because what if we don't? What about your family member? Friend? Neighbor? Coworker? The people in your community, what will happen to these people if they never believe the gospel? Have you had an opportunity to share the gospel with them? Have you made the effort? What about those who have never heard about Jesus? There are over three billion unreached people in the world today. *Unreached* means they have no means to hear and know about Jesus.

Think about these people. If no one goes to them and they never hear about Jesus, then they will spend eternity in hell because they never heard about the only person who can keep them from hell. The terrifying truth is that all these people will spend eternity away from Christ if they never hear the gospel, and if they never believe in the gospel. The motivating truth is that we have the truth, hope, peace, and joy they need and are looking for. We have the gospel of Jesus Christ, and as God's people, we must do everything we can to go and take the good news of the gospel to these people so they can hear, they can believe, and they can spend eternity with Christ as opposed to away from Christ. Let this motivate us to send, to go, and to proclaim the gospel. I want to remind you again that when we go, we do not go alone. God sends us out with His presence and His power through the Holy Spirit. The Holy Spirit empowers us, speaks through us, and He is the one who convicts sins and opens up hearts to receive the gospel. Our only part is to be obedient and go and proclaim. The Holy Spirit's part is to convict. This should give us confidence as we go.

If God's people are to be obedient to the Great Commission, then we must start building relationships with people with the intent of sharing the gospel with them. How do we build a relationship with them? First, it starts with prayer. In Luke 10:2, Jesus was about to send out the seventy-two, but the first thing He told them to do was to pray. As God's people, we must pray for God to send out laborers into the harvest, and we must also pray for God to send us.

We must be praying daily that God would be give us opportunities to meet people, build relationships with them, and have opportunities to share the gospel with them. Matt Queen gives us a great way to pray for opportunities. He stated, "Dear God, give me opportunities to share the gospel today. When they occur, help me recognize them, and give me the courage and boldness to make the most of each opportunity to be able to share the gospel."[124] We must pray boldness when opportunities come. In Acts 4, the apostles were being threatened for preaching the gospel, and in verse 29, they prayed God would give them boldness to continue to proclaim the truth of the gospel in the midst of opposition.

We must pray for God to open up hearts and minds to hear the gospel message and to not only hear the message but to also believe the gospel message. In 2 Corinthians 4:4, the god of this world has blinded the minds of unbelievers, to keep them from believing so we must pray that God would remove their blindness so they can see the truth.

We must pray for salvation. We must pray God would spread His gospel and His kingdom throughout our city and to the nations. One of my favorite books of the Bible and one of my favorite people in the Bible is Nehemiah. When you study the book of Nehemiah, you learn quickly that Nehemiah was a prayer warrior. When Nehemiah hears a report that Jerusalem has been destroyed, the first thing he does is to weep and then pray. In chapter 1 verses 5–11, we see Nehemiah pray for God to forgive His people and to restore them and to restore the city. Nehemiah interceded for the people and for the city. As Christians, we must intercede for our city, our country, and for the nations. We must pray that God would spread the gospel and His kingdom from out city and all over the world.

The book of Nehemiah states how Nehemiah prayed everyday (1:4) and twice a day (1:6). From the time he started to pray to God in chapter 1 (month of Chislev) to the time in chapter 2 when God answered his prayer (month of Nisan), it was about four to five months, so for four to five months. Nehemiah begged God daily and at least twice a day to answer his prayers. Nehemiah knew the power of prayer, and we need to know the power of prayer. Nehemiah prayed daily, and we need to pray daily, and we need to continue praying until God answers our prayers.

Charles Spurgeon stated this about prayer:

---

[124] Matt Queen, *Recapturing Evangelism: A Biblical-Theological Approach* (Brentwood, TN: B&H Publishing, 2023), 18.

> Until the gates of hell is shut upon a man, we must not cease to pray for him. And if we see him hugging the very doorposts of damnation, we must go to the mercy seat and beseech the arm of grace to pluck him from his dangerous position. While there is life there is hope, and although the soul is almost smothered with despair, we must not despair for it, but rather arouse to awaken the Almighty arm.[125]

Thomas Reiner and Steve Parr revealed recently that regardless of their size or location, SBC Churches who report the highest rate of baptisms attribute to their evangelistic effectiveness to praying for the salvation of nonbelievers.[126]

Second, we need to look for opportunities. In Acts 8:26, the Spirit told Phillip to go a desert place where he would meet an Ethiopian eunuch. Phillip was obedient, and he went, and as he approached the man, the man was reading Isaiah 53. Phillip was able to lead him to the truth where he became a believer. We need to always be looking for where God is working, and we need to always be open to when the Spirit puts people into our lives in or to have gospel conversations with them.

Third, we need to be truthful. As we seek to live on mission, we must be truthful with people. If we really want to be loving to people, then we must be truthful with them. We must be truthful about the seriousness and the destruction of sin. We must be truthful in that living anyway that is outside God's design will only lead to destruction personally and in the society. We must be truthful in that we must not seek anything other than Jesus for our hope, peace, joy, and satisfaction because only Jesus can give us these things, and anything else will only lead us to destruction. We must also speak truth about the good news of the gospel. The good news of the gospel is

---

[125] Matt Queen, *Recapturing Evangelism* (Brentwood, TN: B & H Academic, 2023), 147.
[126] Ibid., 144.

that Jesus Christ came and died on the cross so that we can be saved, forgiven of our sins, freed from our sins, and have a relationship with God and live with Him forever in His kingdom. The gospel of Jesus is the only thing that will truly give us peace, hope, and joy. The gospel is the only thing that will give us true satisfaction and the only thing that will give us life and human flourishing.

As we seek to live on mission, we must engage people with the whole gospel. We must preach a Jesus who loves, and we must preach a Jesus who judges. The world loves and has no problem with a Jesus who loves, but the world wants nothing to do with a Jesus who judges. We must preach repentance and confession of sins. We must preach a surrendering of our lives to Jesus and surrender to His Lordship in all our lives. We must preach dying to ourselves daily and living in a way that pleases and honors Jesus every day. We must preach the truth about hell in that those who deny Jesus as their Lord and Savior will spend eternity away from Jesus in hell where there will be eternal punishment.

Fourth, we need to show love and compassion. Although we must be truthful, we must also be loving. In John 8, these Jewish leaders brought a woman caught in adultery to Jesus, where the punishment for this is stoning. Jesus told the men that whoever is without sin cast the first stone. The men leave, and Jesus told the woman that He did not condemn her, and He told her to go and sin no more. Jesus was truthful with this woman, but He also showed her love and compassion as He did not condemn her. The church historically has been very truthful but not very loving. I have met many people who have been hurt greatly by the church because the church has been judgmental and condemning to them and has not been loving.

In the book *God Delusion* by Richard Dawkins, who is an atheist, he said that he gets lots of letters. Some people praise him, some question him, and some hate him; and he said the most hateful letters he gets come from Christians. He even gives some examples:

> Hello, Cheese-eating scumbag. There are way more of us Christians than you losers. There is no separation of church and state and you hea-

thens will lose. You Satan worshipping scum. I hope you die and go to hell. I hope you get a painful disease like cancer and die a slow painful death, so you can meet your god, Satan.[127]

Imagine this is coming from someone who claims to be a Jesus follower.

As we seek to live on a mission, we must be truthful, but we must also be loving and compassionate because Jesus was truthful yet loving and compassionate. If Christians really want to reach lost people with the good news of the gospel, then we must show them love and compassion because if we do not show them love, how can we expect them to listen to the truth? How can we expect to tell someone how Jesus loves them and then at the same time show them hate and be condemning? The truth is that we cannot. We must show them the love of Jesus with our words and with our actions. I truly believe that if we first show them love, then they will listen to our message.

Fifth, we need to disciple them. The Great Commission commands us to go and make disciples, so if we want to truly fulfill the Great Commission, then we must go and make disciples. The truth is that when Jesus gave us the Great Commission, He did not give it to a special group of people. No, Jesus gave the Great Commission to all Christians. The moment you became a Christian was the moment you were given the Great Commission, and we must all be obedient to it by going and making disciples. If we want to fulfill the Great Commission and get the good news of the gospel to those who have yet to hear, then we must all go and be disciple makers and make disciples to all nations. These were the last words that Jesus gave us before He went to be with the Father, and we better be ready for His return. The way we get prepared is by being a disciple and living the way He desires us to and to be a disciples maker and go and make

---

[127] Richard Dawkins, *The God Delusion* (New York, NY: HarperCollins Publishers, 2008), 243.

disciples. Are you currently being prepared for the return of Jesus? Who are you discipling right now?

As this book comes to a close, here is my challenge and my prayer for you: My challenge is that you would take some time, sit down, and write down everyone in your life who you feel needs to know the truth of the gospel. Once you write down these people, begin to pray for them. Pray God would give you an opportunity to get to know them, build a relationship with them, and pray God would give you an opportunity to share the gospel with them and disciple them. After you have prayed for these opportunities, now think and write out a plan where you can begin to get to know them for the purpose of building a relationship with them that prayerfully leads to the opportunity to share the gospel with them and disciple them. Take one step at a time but know that God is with you every step of the way. My prayer is that as you do this, God will show up in a mighty way and use you to build relationships with those in your life and use you to tell them about Jesus and to help make them faithful disciples of Jesus. Be encouraged and go and make disciples of all nations.

Bibliography

Anderson, Chris. *The God Who Satisfies: How Jesus Seeks, Saves and Satisfies Samaritan Woman—Like Us.* Church Works, 2016.

Anyabwile, Thabiti. *Christ-Centered Exposition: Luke.* Nashville: B&H Publishing, 2018.

Ashford, Bruce Riley. *Every Square Inch: An Introduction to Cultural Engagement for Christians.* Bellingham: Lexham Press, 2015.

Barrs, Jerram. *Learning Evangelism from Jesus.* Wheaton: Crossway, 2009.

Bennett, Matthew. *Hope for American Evangelicals: A Missionary Perspective on Restoring our Broken House.* Brentwood: B&H Publishing, 2023.

Beougher, Timothy. *Invitation to Evangelism: Sharing the Gospel with Compassion and Conviction.* Grand Rapids: Kregel Academic, 2021.

Brady, Tom. Interview with Tom Brady. *60 Minutes*, November 5, 2005. https://www.cbsnews.com/news/transcript-tom-brady-part-3/.

Butterfield, Rosaria. "My Train Wreck Conversion," *Christianity Today*, February 7, 2013, accessed http://www.christianitytoday.com/ct/2013/january-february/my-train-wreck-conversion.html.

Butterfield, Rosaria. *The Gospel Comes with a House Key: Practicing Radically Ordinary Hospitality in Our Post-Christian World.* Wheaton: Crossway, 2018.

Calvin, John. *Commentary on the Gospel According to John*, vol 1. Grand Rapids: Baker Books, 1999.

Carson, D. A. *The Gospel According to John*. Grand Rapids: Eerdmans Publishing, 1991.

Carter, Matt, and Josh Wredburg. *Christ-Centered Exposition: John*. Nashville: B&H Publishing, 2017.

Chandler, Matt. Desiring God Conference for Pastors, 2009.

Chatraw, Joshua D. *Telling a Better Story: How to Talk About God in a Skeptical Age*. Grand Rapids: Zondervan Academics, 2020.

Chester, Tim. *A Meal with Jesus: Discovering Grace, Community and Mission Around the Table*. Wheaton: Crossway, 2011.

Chester, Tim, and Steve Timmis. *Total Church*. Wheaton: Crossway, 2008.

Dawkins, Richard. *The God Delusion*. New York: HarpersCollins Publishers, 2008.

Evans, Tony. *Oneness Embraced: Reconciliation, the Kingdom, and How We Are Stronger Together*. Chicago: Moody Publishers, 2011.

Garrow, David. *Bearing the Cross*. New York: Harper Collins Publishers, 1986.

Geisler, David, and Norman Geisler. *Conversational Evangelism: Connecting with People to Share Jesus*. Eugene: Harvest House Publishing, 2014.

Goodmanson, Drew. "Gospel Hospitality: Making Room," Kaleo Church, San Diego, September 2, 2007, accessed www.kaleo-church.com/sermon/gospel-hospitality-making-room.

Greear, J. D. "The Next Wave of Missions," *J.D. Greear Ministries*, accessed December 2, 2011, http://jdgreear.com/blog/the-next-wave-of-missions/.

Green, Michael. *Evangelism in the Early Church*, rev. ed. Grand Rapids: Eerdmans, 2003.

Greer, Sam. *The Gospel Conversation: Engaging the Lost in Everyday Life*. Replicate, 2017.

Greer, Sam. *The Gospel Conversationalist*. Bloomington: Zondervan, 2018.

Hamilton, Andrew. "Food and Friends Night," Backyardmissionary.com (blog), June 14, 2006, www.backyardmissionary.com.

Horton, D. A. *Intentional: Kingdom Ethnicity in a Divided World*. Colorado Springs: NAVPress, 2019.

Hughes, Kent. *Preaching the Word: John*. Wheaton: Crossway, 1999.

Hughes, Kent. *Preaching the Word: Luke*. Wheaton: Crossway, 2015.

Jillette, Penn. "A Gift of a Bible." YouTube video. https://youtu.be/6md638smQd8.

Keller, Tim. *Ministries of Mercy*, 3rd ed. Phillipsburg: P&R Publishing, 2015.

Keller, Tim. *Making Sense of God: An Invitation to the Skeptical*. New York: Penguin Random House, 2016.

King, Martin Luther, Jr. "Letter from a Birmingham Jail," in Milestone Documents in African American History by Paul Murray. Armenia: Salem Press, 2017.

MacArthur, John. *The MacArthur New Testament Commentary: John 1–11*. Chicago: Moody Publishers, 2006.

Mcdowell, Bruce A. and Anees Zaka. *Muslims and Christians at the Table: Promoting Biblical Understanding among North American Muslims*. Phillisburg: P&R Publishing, 1999.

Milne, Bruce. *The Bible Speaks Today: The Message of John*, John Stott, ed. Downers Grove: IVP Academic, 1981.

Newbigin, Lesslie. *A Word in Season*. Grand Rapids: Eerdmans Publishing, 1994.

Oldenburg, Ray. *The Great Good Place: Cafes, Coffee Shops, Bookstores, Bars, Hair Salons, and Other Hangouts at the Heart of a Community*. Philadelphia: Da Capo, 1999.

Paton, John. *John G. Paton: The Autobiography of the Pioneer Missionary to the New Hebrides*. Banner of Truth, 2013.

Perkins, John. *Dream with Me: Race, Love, and the Struggle We Must Win*. Grand Rapids: Baker Books, 2017.

Piper, John. *Desiring God*. Sisters: Multnomah Publishers, 2003.

Piper, John. *Let the Nations Be Glad: The Supremacy of God in Missions*. Grand Rapids: Baker Academic, 2022.

Platt, David. "A Testimony Worth Telling: John 4:39," Radical: Pray the Word. August 13, 2019. https://radical.net/podcasts/pray-the-word/a-testimony-worth-telling-john-439/.

Putnam, Robert. *Bowling Alone*: Simon & Schuster, 2000.

Queen, Matt. *Recapturing Evangelism*. Brentwood: B&H Publishing, 2023.

Reeder, Caryn. *The Samaritan Woman's Story*. Downers Grove: InterVarsity Press, 2022.

Rohl, Christine. D. *Making Room: Recovering Hospitality as a Christian Tradition*. Grand Rapids: Eerdmans, 1999.

Ryle, JC. *Expository Thoughts on the Gospels*. Vol. 3. Grand Rapids: Baker Books, 2007.

St. Augustine of Hippo, *The Confessions: With an Introduction and Contemporary Criticism*, ed. David Vincent Meconi. San Francisco: Ignatius, 2012.

Schreiner, Patrick. *Political Gospel: Public Witness in a Politically Crazy World*. Brentwood: B&H Publishing, 2023.

Sharp, Larry. *Missions Disrupted*. Peabody: Hendrickson Publishing, 2022.

Trueblood, Elton. *The Company of the Committed*. HarperCollins, 1979.

Tsague, Patrick. "What Is a Kingdom Business?" *Regent University Center for Entrepreneurship*. https://regententrepreneur.org/what-is-kingdom-business/.

Turner, Harvey. *Friends of Sinners: An Approach to Evangelism*. Houston: Lucid Books, 2016.

Uplifting Education. "Consequences of the Sexual Revolution." https://www.upliftingeducation.com/consequences-of-the-sexual-revolution.

Wesley, John. Letter from Wesley to Wilberforce on February 24, 1791, https://medium.com/@rickhogaboam/john-wesleys-final-letter-to-william-wilberforce-slavery-and-the-sanctity-of-life-571538291c16.

Williams, Dustin, and Brandon College. *The Simplest Way to Change the World: Biblical Hospitality as a Way of Life*. Chicago: Moody Publishers, 2017.

Williams, Jarvis. *One New Man: The Cross and Racial Reconciliation in Pauline Theology*. Nashville: B&H Publishing, 2010.

Willis, Dustin, and Aaron Coe. *Life on Mission: Joining the Everyday Mission of God*. Chicago: Moody Publishers, 2014.

About the Author

Patrick Sawyer currently serves as the missional living pastor at Valleydale Church in Birmingham, Alabama. Patrick holds a master of divinity from Southeastern Baptist Theological Seminary. He is currently pursuing a doctor of philosophy from Midwestern Baptist Theological Seminary. His passion is to encourage and equip Christians to live on mission daily where they live, work, and play.

Prior to full-time ministry, Patrick worked in the business world in the athletic training profession. As a certified athletic trainer, he served in many different settings such as high school, college, and sports marketing. Patrick holds a bachelor's degree from Auburn University and a master's degree from the University of Kentucky.

He's been married to Dawn since 2004 and has one son, Connor. They currently live in Birmingham, Alabama.